Praise for
Theology: Mythos or Logos?

"John Médaille and Thomas Storck have done a wonderful thing in this book. In a time when mere partisan yarking across no-man's-lands of intellectual barrenness passes for a 'national conversation,' these men revive the true meaning of the word 'argue': that is, to clarify. Read this book and profit from two thoughtful minds in pursuit of truth, goodness, and beauty."—MARK SHEA, author of *The Church's Best-Kept Secret*

"Two Catholic scholars and friends reflect together on the *Euthyphro* of Plato, relating its arguments to Christian faith and both divine and natural revelation. In the course of their cordial 'debate' they discuss the perennial issue of the relationship of philosophy, with its abstract approach to truth, to the Christian 'story,' mythos, and history. The exchanges are warm, insightful, charitable, and provide a model of how two different intellectual approaches to the Catholic faith can converge in essential unity while maintaining the integrity of each approach. There is much to chew on here and this winsome little book is sure to engage the thoughtful reader."—ADDISON HODGES HART, author of *Confessions of the Anti-Christ*

"Ever since the dialogue of Socrates and Euthyphro, *Logos* has had the upper hand over *Mythos* in Western culture. In *Theology: Mythos or Logos?*, John Médaille, taking the mystical approach to epistemology, argues that, in fact, *Mythos* is fundamental and *Logos* follows, that poetry grounds philosophy and story dictates science. Thomas Storck, taking the scholastic approach to epistemology, retorts that reason must ground faith, stories must be judged by science, and philosophy uncovers truth, not poetry. Reading this conversation, I find my sympathies flow back and forth between the positions, as both argue their case rigorously and persuasively. Any reader of this book will find their epistemological foundations shaken but their thinking enriched as Médaille and Storck delve ever more deeply into how we know and how we believe."—ROMAN A. MONTERO, author of *All Things in Common: The Economic Practices of the Early Christians*, and *Jesus's Manifesto: The Sermon on the Plain*

"Is there a neutral space where believer and non-believer can reason together about the existence of God? Do we err in even attempting to make the historical case for the resurrection? In this wonderfully thought-provoking dialogue, distinguished Catholic thinkers John Médaille and Thomas Storck present two radically opposing answers to these questions, two radically opposing views of the place of faith, reason, and history in Christian apologetics. For anyone interested in the question of where our modern world has gone wrong and what sort of apologetic is needed to win it back, this book is pure gold."—KENNETH HENSLEY, Catholic apologist, Pastoral Care Coordinator for Coming Home Network, and co-author of *The Godless Delusion*

"Beginning in 2018, John Médaille and Thomas Storck began an exchange of letters, collected here, ranging over issues of faith, reason, history, economics, politics, and social philosophy. They wrote as friends and from the perspective of their shared Catholic faith, but with very different philosophical commitments. They disagreed, sometimes sharply, but did so out of an ultimate concern for truth and wholeness. In this, they have provided a model of how substantive, Christian conversation—and argument!—might proceed in a time when concern for clarity, conviction, care, and above all, charity seems so rare."—THE REV. JASON A. FOUT, Bexley Seabury Seminary Federation, Chicago, IL

Theology: Mythos or Logos?

A Dialogue on Faith, Reason, and History

Theology: Mythos or Logos?

A Dialogue on
Faith, Reason, and History

$\oplus$

John Médaille
&
Thomas Storck

Foreword by
Philipp W. Rosemann

❧ Angelico Press

First published in the
USA by Angelico Press
© John Médaille and Thomas Storck 2020
Foreword © Philipp W. Rosemann 2020

For information, address:
Angelico Press
169 Monitor St.
Brooklyn, NY 11222
angelicopress.com

ISBN 978-1-62138-663-6 (pbk)
ISBN 978-1-62138-664-3 (cloth)
ISBN 978-1-62138-665-0 (ebook)

Cover Design: Michael Schrauzer

Foreword

Philipp W. Rosemann

T HERE IS A RISK in writing a foreword to a book—
indeed, in writing anything that is meant to be of
more than momentary, journalistic value—in a man-
ner that is too personal or too topical. But I will run this risk
here, and I will do so not least because one of the many
strengths of John Médaille and Thomas Storck's book is to
shed light upon an important aspect of our current plight.

The "current plight" I want to speak of is the deplorable
state of the American republic. If there is anything the so-
called "left" and the so-called "right" are able to agree on, it is
the fact that the American political space is completely frac-
tured, to such an extent that the inhabitants of this space no
longer appear to be capable of engaging in meaningful dialogue. For meaningful dialogue requires some basis, some
starting point—like an agreed set of facts about which to disagree. Americans, however, seem to inhabit parallel uni-
verses with increasingly little factual overlap. This situation
has been in the making for some time, it is true, but Donald
Trump's presidency and the outbreak of the coronavirus have
brought it to a head. To some, Trump is a genius, a savior; to
others, he is a narcissistic monster. To some, we are living a
health crisis of historic dimensions that has been exacerbated
by the monster's incompetence; to others, the "health crisis"
has to be placed in quotation marks, since—hardly worse
than the flu—it represents but a ploy of the global elite to

1

deprive citizens of their liberties and prevent the reelection of the savior.

I am fortunate enough to be a citizen of two worlds: in other words, I have friends—people whom I dearly love and respect—in both of these camps. This means that I find it hard to take sides in the strident and unambiguous way that is characteristic of most of my contemporaries. Instead, I would like to do what I can to surmount the opposition, by identifying some common ground; but, first of all, I want to understand what exactly is happening in this collapse of discourse, this fracturing of the political space.

And there it is again: the word "space." It plays an important role in John and Thomas's book, when the two authors, in their dialogue, digging deeper and deeper toward the foundations of their disagreement, wonder how dialogue is possible at all. Thomas Storck argues that there is a common space of reason that is shared by all human beings. This does not mean, of course, that all rational people will spontaneously agree on all important matters—the most important matter being the existence of God and the content of religious faith. It does mean, on the other hand, that there are common principles to be applied and a logic to be followed in ascertaining truth. All disagreements, then, are ultimately due to the fact that one side has failed to reason correctly, perhaps under the influence of passion or prejudice.

John Médaille submits that such a neutral space of reason is the pernicious invention of modern liberalism. This liberalism creates a secular rationality that deprives human beings of their most precious ground: the deeply meaningful religious "stories" which alone are able to give moral orientation to their lives. These stories, however, are not reducible to rational arguments. This is obvious in the case of religious

2

narratives, but applies even to science, which ultimately rests upon assumptions and beliefs. John's argument represents a typically "postmodern" move: philosophers since Hegel have held that reason, rather than being timeless, is inextricably connected with (hi)story. If we follow John's line of thinking, we will have to conclude that coherent systems of thought— be they religious, philosophical, or scientific—can never be defeated from the outside; they will be refuted, if at all, only through internal weaknesses that will appear over time to the adherents of these systems, forcing them to reconsider.

What happens when we apply these two conceptions of reason to the Christian faith? That is the central issue this book addresses. The contrasting visions that emerge can be summed up in two biblical quotations that keep recurring in the dialogue of our authors.

In arguing for the fundamental reasonableness of the faith, Thomas Storck appeals to Romans 1:19–21:

> For what can be known about God is plain to them, because God has shown it to them. Ever since the creation of the world his eternal power and divine nature, invisible though they are, have been understood and seen through the things he has made. So they are without excuse; for though they knew God, they did not honor him as God or give thanks to him, but they became futile in their thinking, and their senseless minds were darkened. (NRSV)

Many of the elements of Thomas's position are present in this short text. Any person who is not "senseless," St. Paul is arguing here, whose mind is not clouded by moral defect, can understand at the very least that there is a God, a Creator. Thomas goes further: even central tenets of the faith, such as the Resurrection, are subject to rational scrutiny of their historical veracity. If this were not the case, then why would the same Paul, in his First Letter to the Corinthians (1 Cor 15:6), stress that the risen Lord has appeared to no fewer than five hundred brothers, many still alive at the time? To be sure, it is possible to question the value of such testimony, but any rational person will have to weigh this evidence very carefully. Thus, without denying the narrative elements in the two Testaments, Thomas is not willing to regard them as merely two sets of appealing and interesting "stories." Stories are not enough to move anyone to rational assent.

John Médaille opens this book with another Pauline text, also drawn from the First Letter to the Corinthians. It has a very different tone:

> Consider your own call, brothers and sisters: not many of you were wise by human standards, not many were powerful, not many were of noble birth. But God chose what is foolish in the world to shame the wise; God chose what is weak in the world to shame the strong. (1 Cor 1:26–27, NRSV)

The context of the quotation clarifies which aspect of the faith, in particular, Paul has in mind when he prizes Christian "foolishness" over worldly wisdom: "For Jews demand signs and Greeks desire wisdom, but we proclaim Christ crucified, a stumbling block to Jews and foolishness to Gentiles" (1 Cor 1:22–23; NRSV). According to St. Paul, it is specifically the Cross that defies human wisdom: the death of the Son of God, who allowed himself to be tortured to death like an abject criminal. The logic at work in the life of the *Logos*, John Médaille would argue, is not the logic of philosophic reason. Understanding this logic, rather, requires listening to the Gospel accounts of Jesus's life; it requires entering into the biography of the God-man, having faith in his promises, following in his footsteps. Such faithful fellowship is what John feels leads to conversion (of others as much as of oneself): it is the appeal of Jesus's "story" that converts, not anyone's Five Ways to prove God's existence. Religion is personal commitment, prayer, ritual, sacrifice—not ratiocination. This is why John terms his approach "mystical," distinguishing it from Thomas's "scholastic" method.

"Thomas's scholastic method"! Which Thomas are we talking about here? Two, at least, for Thomas Storck is an ardent follower of his namesake, St. Thomas Aquinas. For Thomas, St. Thomas exemplifies the rational approach to the faith that he champions in his dialogue with John Médaille. Without denying the supernatural elements of the faith, Aquinas spent a lifetime demonstrating that the Christian faith is rational; it is faith in the *Logos* become flesh. Christians can offer *proof* of God's existence and *compelling reasons* for belief in central tenets of the faith like the Resurrection. Thomas Storck finds strong evidence for the power of this approach in the flourishing of Catholic culture that occurred in the wake of the encyclical *Aeterni Patris*, in which Pope Leo XIII commended Thomism as the Catholic answer to secular modernity. As long as the Church was guided by Thomas's thought—in which the great tradition of perennial philosophy, from Thales onwards, culminates—it commanded respect and exercised significant intellectual appeal. By contrast, it is not an accident that the decline of Thomism in the second half of the twentieth century was paralleled by a decline of the hold of the Church on human culture, from politics and economics to personal morality.

And who is Thomas Aquinas for John Médaille? Not the answer to secular modernity, but its cause! For John, there is a direct line running from Aquinas to Descartes, from the rationalism of scholastic method to the scientism of modernity, even to the secular space of disembodied, unhistorical reason. Nonetheless, overall John views modernity in more favorable terms than Thomas does. John feels that many of the accomplishments of the modern age, including even a certain type of liberalism, have their roots in the Middle Ages. In particular, the Christian discovery of the supreme value and dignity of the individual began to produce rich fruit in the medieval period. Thus, within natural law the notion of natural rights developed, and Christian communities where spiritual ties transcended the limitations of birth and blood—monasteries—practiced forms of democratic governance. With canon law, a body of law came into existence that applied to all Christians, irrespective of origin or social standing. On John's reading, then, the modern project has roots in the Middle Ages in both its strengths and its weaknesses. Thomas, by contrast, defends the view that modernity sprang from the poisonous root of nominalism, whose denial of universals led to the collapse of the metaphysical order, which was replaced by a primacy of will over reason. The divorce of faith from reason logically ensued, exposing Christianity to the risk of appearing like one subjective choice amongst others. Modernity, therefore, is something the Church must oppose and overcome, not accommodate. The sound teachings of St. Thomas Aquinas are the best instrument to accomplish this task.

My role as author of this foreword is not, thankfully, to adjudicate between the two visions that Thomas Storck and John Médaille advocate so eloquently in this book—visions encompassing the nature of reason in relation to history, the relationship between reason and faith, and the right attitude of the Church toward modernity, to mention only the most prominent topics. Indeed, I almost have the impression that John and Thomas's amicable debate replicates some of the traits of the political impasse that I sketched at the outset: two intelligent people, men of undoubted goodwill, come to fundamentally different conclusions in thinking about an important subject. So, it seems as though we have come full circle and must address, all over again, the question of the space in which meaningful conversation is able to occur.

Fortunately, there are several lessons to be drawn from John and Thomas's conversation. The first lesson, perhaps, stems from the fact that their dialogue did in fact occur— even if, in the end, neither of the two managed to convince the other. Why was the dialogue able to occur, and why did the participants persist in it (even though, every now and then, the reader catches a hint, just between the lines, of mild exasperation)? I venture a twofold answer. First, there is the undoubted goodwill of the two men involved. They make an honest effort to listen, opening themselves to the possibility of being challenged. They expose their views— indeed themselves—to "difference" (to employ, just once, that overused postmodern term). Second, I suspect that this openness to the arguments of the other has a twofold root: a friendship already established well before the conversation, and the shared Christian faith of the interlocutors. These last two points are connected, at least to an extent: not all Christians will easily become friends (alas, given the instructions of our Lord), but a shared foundation is a good starting point for a meaningful human relationship.

A shared foundation, then, appears crucial for the possibility of dialogue. Neither John nor Thomas questions the Christian faith; rather, the object of their conversation is to deepen that faith, to understand more precisely its meaning and its implications. To be sure, in principle dialogue should be possible with any other human being, simply upon the basis of our shared humanity. In practice, however, dialogue is greatly facilitated the more solid the foundation is to which the interlocutors are able to appeal. (But then again, sometimes vicious fights break out over minute details in small, tight-knit communities. Perhaps we can attribute this unfortunate phenomenon to human fallenness.)

Beyond a common foundation, dialogue requires a method. Interestingly, the starting point of Thomas Storck and John Médaille's exchange of letters is John's interpretation of a Platonic dialogue, the *Euthyphro*, which has Socrates engage his interlocutor about the nature of piety. In the Socratic dialogues, the philosopher invariably ends up exposing deep flaws in the arguments of those whom he questions. Often enough, he embarrasses them (the Athenians' hostility toward Socrates did not come from nowhere). One would perhaps go too far in claiming that Socrates does not take his interlocutors seriously; yet there is never a doubt as to who is in charge, who will have the last word (or laugh). It is clear, therefore, that the Platonic dialogue is not the ideal blueprint for the kind of dialogue which Thomas and John are modeling in their book.

The kind of conversation conducted in this book is philosophical, to be sure, but it is also Christian. Now as it happens, a method of Christian intellectual dialogue does not have to be invented; it already exists. The scholastic method, whose emergence and gradual perfection since the time of the Church Fathers was first chronicled by the great German medievalist Fr. Martin Grabmann, relied on a sophisticated combination of intellectual techniques to allow for an increasing penetration and elucidation of the Christian faith, along with (or even through) the incorporation of non-Christian ideas into the Christian tradition. While scholastic method always remained guided by the goal to serve Christian thought, it was remarkably bold in entertaining even the most radical objections to the faith, as well as every possible shade of Christian opinion. We see evidence of this boldness in Aquinas's willingness to consider arguments against the existence of God. The very first sentence that opens the famous article of the *Summa* where Aquinas sketches the Five Ways (*Summa theologiae* I, qu. 2, art. 3) reads, "It seems that God does not exist."

The mental habit of the scholastic thinker was such that he considered every question in terms of the contradictory answers that it could elicit. Peter Abelard called this method *sic et non*, "yes and no," or "pro and con." The next step in this method was to seek out the strongest arguments for the contradictory views. The juxtaposition and explanation of these arguments was followed by an attempt to understand where their authors were "coming from," as we would say. Why on earth, for example, would anyone deny that God exists? Why would anyone subscribe to an Arian conception of the Son of God? Or identify charity with the Holy Spirit (rather than regarding it as an infused virtue)? Doing justice to all the arguments required distinctions: if one looked at the issue from a certain perspective—limited, partial—then indeed one might arrive at a view which, when the matter was considered more comprehensively, turned out to be erroneous. The objective of the scholastic thinker was to identify these perspectives and, through them and beyond them, arrive at a more comprehensive solution.

Aquinas's *Summa theologiae* is the quintessential illustration of exactly that method. In bringing it to bear on the Christian faith, Aquinas was open to incorporating material from the entire breadth of the Western tradition, including—to some contemporaries, scandalously so—many ideas of the pagan Aristotle and his Jewish and Muslim followers.

The scholastic method, the method employed by St. Thomas and so many others, is far from being a product of the Middle Ages that is now of merely academic interest.[†] It even seems to me that it could be an inspiration to address some of the deep divisions in the American political landscape. If the proponents of radically opposing views would only listen to each other with a modicum of goodwill, much would already be gained. If, moreover, they would consider from what perspective the arguments of the other side were formulated, which aspect of reality or even just of human experience they might reflect, further understanding would be reached. And if, finally, political discourse were conceived as the attempt of rational people of goodwill to move toward an always greater truth, one that is never exhausted by a single point of view, then there would be hope—hope, not that all political differences would finally be overcome, but that through respect for the opinions of others a space for meaningful political conversation would once again open up in America.

August 2020
The National University of Ireland, Maynooth

[†] I point here to a small book that Joseph Ratzinger edited when he was a professor at the University of Regensburg. Under the title, *Aktualität der Scholastik* (Regensburg: Pustet, 1975), it brings together contributions by several authors who argue for the present-day interest of the scholastic approach. Josef Pieper's piece is (no surprise) particularly compelling.

Absurd Wisdom:
An Apology for Euthyphro†

John Médaille

Not many of you are wise, as men account wisdom.…
God chose those whom the world considers absurd to
shame the wise. (1 Cor 1:26–27)

The Philosopher and the Theologian

The *Euthyphro* of Plato is among the earliest recorded
accounts of the dialogue between the philosophers and the
theologians, of the conflict between reason and faith. The
"wisdom" Euthyphro receives from the gods through the
poetry of Hesiod and Homer is challenged by the wisdom
available to the "natural" reason, as manifested in the probing
questions of Socrates. Euthyphro, who claims to know more
of these matters than the ordinary run of men, is shown to
know very little when subjected to the test; the contradictions in his position, derived from poetry, will not stand up
to the questioning of philosophy, derived from reason alone.
And yet, it is fair to ask whether we, as Christians, can so
blithely accept Euthyphro's defeat when we ourselves, and in
our own literature, bear equally the charge of contradiction
on a daily basis. Can we accept so easily a faith that is bound

---

† Originally published at *Front Porch Republic*, October 15, 2018. The
complete dialogue by Plato is included below as an Appendix.

by reason, and must we deny to theology its own methods and sources, apart from philosophy? Speaking as a theologian, I find it necessary to defend the art of our guild, even when practiced by one so artless as Euthyphro.

Whichever "wisdom" will "win," the *Euthyphro* is a carefully constructed work of literature rich in its use of irony. Euthyphro and Socrates, the seer and the sage, are both drawn to the court by issues of impiety, one to make such a charge and one to be so charged. The irony is compounded by the fact that the seer is present to prosecute his own father, a most impious act in the eyes of his countrymen. Seeing that Euthyphro knows enough about piety to commit such an act, Socrates becomes his student, somewhat disingenuously, in order to learn some defense for his own trial, and Euthyphro promises to help him. But the sage is able to learn little from the seer, despite the fact that Euthyphro offers no less than seven definitions of piety. All are found wanting by the philosopher, who begins with a rejection of the poets upon whom Euthyphro depends. In the end, the irony is made complete as the befuddled theologian departs the court, abandoning both the threatened prosecution of his father and the promised defense of Socrates; the philosopher meanwhile remains to face his own trial alone, without the help of revealed theology. Human wisdom alone must carry the day, as it has already carried off the theologian.

The Wisdom of Socrates

Socrates's critique of Euthyphro turns on three questions: the believability of the myths, the unity of the lovely and what is actually loved by the gods, and the unity of justice and holiness. The first question is actually the basis of his own trial; he tells us that because he rejects the myths, people believe him to be sinful. Socrates seeks only the "essential form" of the holy and the unholy, not their poetic representations. Poetry is a bad place to search for essential forms, for poetry moves us by metaphor through the particular towards ideas it assumes to be otherwise inexpressible.

The unity of the lovely and what is loved by the gods is also rejected, and not without support of the poets themselves. Since the gods war with each other, they cannot agree on what is good; hence there must be different goods to different gods. And just as clearly the good must be something apart from the gods; hence the opinion of the gods cannot count for more than the opinion of men; the gods might be powerful, but they are not thereby truthful. Men must be able to grasp the truth apart from the myths, and this is especially true as the Muses themselves are prone to lying; man must develop his own wisdom, since he cannot trust the wisdom of the Muse. Further, since the gods may love what is not good, then the good precedes the gods and stands above them and ought to rule them, just as the philosophers ought to rule the state. This is the "good" at which Socrates aims, whether or not it is loved by one, all, or none of the gods.

Aside from dividing truth from poetry and the good from the gods, Socrates divides justice and holiness. The service of the gods and the service of men become two clear and distinct things, only one of which involves piety. This service of the gods is conceived to be in the same class as the service of horses or of dogs, something done to improve them. But since neither party can agree to such a thing, the dialogue degenerates, until "piety" becomes no more than an exchange of goods, sacrifices to the gods in exchange for blessings on the family and the state. Thus piety at best becomes a divine commerce, neither more nor less noble than that which takes place in the *agora*. Against this, Euthyphro can only re-assert his original definition; threatened by Socrates with repeating the conversation from the beginning, the theologian flees the scene, abandoning both father and philosopher to their fates, and the philosopher must continue alone.

It is this search for the essence of the good, apart from its shifting expression in the world of "things," that compels the reason that is at the heart of the wisdom of Socrates. His method, as we have seen, is the method of analysis, of continually dividing things until their indivisible elements are reached, along with the chain of causes that connects them. In this way, Socrates gets to the essential form of all things, which is found to be the pure and pre-existing ideas. Moreover, he subjects not only the theologian to such analysis, but the statesman, the poet, and the artist as well; all are found lacking in wisdom, all have failed in proper analytic technique. The knowledge that Socrates seeks is *objective*, since only an object may be analyzed; the subjective remains always either slightly beyond reach, or beneath it. Indeed, the gods themselves must be subjected, like all else, to the test; no longer are they active *subjects* whom men must seek to placate, but *objects*, like everything else, to be analyzed. The analysis does them ill; in the end, it is only the philosopher who is fit to govern; indeed, it is only the philosopher who is fit even to breed, or at least direct the breeding of others. Nor is it an easy task to overthrow this reasoning, however uneasy it may make us feel. For the logic of the pure ideas is indeed compelling in the face of the confusing complexity and changeability of the real world. This leads us directly to the question, "Is there a wisdom apart from philosophy, or is everything, even the gods, subject to its analysis?" In other words, does the "natural" theology of the philosophers bind even God?

"Natural" Theology

When the philosophers search for God, they tend to find him among the pure ideas, or to conceive him as the immutable "unmoved mover." That these ideas flow irresistibly from the logic is undeniable. However, in what sense they are "natural" is another matter. If we assert that they are "natural" in the sense of compelling the rational belief of all men, then it must be pointed out that such ideas are the exception among men, rather than the rule. Hymns to the pure ideas are rather rare, and liturgies that invoke the *primum mobile* are not well attended. Even in religions that accord these ideas a great deal of respect, such as Christianity, their place is mainly confined to the higher realms of theology and they rarely intrude themselves on the liturgical or prayer life of the community. It may be that they are "natural" in the sense that the transuranic elements are natural; that is, they certainly express possible relationships in the order of nature, but are not actually found in the natural world outside the laboratory and only when created by the hand of man. Must we then abandon the idea of a natural theology, or limit its reach to the philosophers?

But there does seem to be a "natural theology" which *has* in fact compelled belief from all men, whether peasant or philosopher, or at least from all cultures. However, this theology is reachable not by the tools of philosophy *per se*, but by the tools of theology, oddly enough. Specifically, it is reachable by applying the Vincentian canon ("that which is always and everywhere believed") to the entire world and to all of its traditions. The canon is designed as a test for Christian tradi-

15

tion, but works as well for tradition in general. When we apply this canon, we find something remarkable. We find that all peoples believe certain things about the divine, among which are that the divinity is reached by prayer, ritual, and sacrifice, and that it is spoken of primarily through poetry and metaphor. This is really a counter-intuitive result, especially if one's intuitions have been formed by philosophy. For there seems to be no chain of reasoning, starting with any arbitrary "first principles" you like, that ends in the conclusion, "and then you place a lamb on the altar and kill it." Indeed, the "rational" mind has a great deal of difficulty connecting the dead lamb to the living God, and yet that is what all peoples do, or something very like it. It may be, as Socrates seems to suspect, that such things are the product of ignorance. Yet, given the ubiquitous nature of the belief, this explanation seems flawed; one would expect correct reasoning to always reach the same result, while ignorance and error would always march off in all sorts of different directions. But it is the philosophers who can't seem to agree, while the mass of men is united on these very points. The very fact that all men seem compelled to do these things and to think in these ways indicates that there is something "natural" in man that compels him thus, even when his intellect, by itself, would rebel at the thought. I suspect that this "natural" thing in man is his power to integrate not only his thoughts but also his experience of the holy. For man must not only analyze, he must also synthesize and, mostly, he must act. And the power of man that allows him to integrate all of the diverse elements that the philosophers divide is his experience of the holy, something he experiences mainly as a lack. It is the discovery of the "empty space" within himself that leads every man to kneel at the altar while offering sacrifice and repeating words that are poetic. It is not something "deduced" from first principles, but something to which man's ordinary experience seems to compel him.

The Wisdom of Euthyphro

It is to this "natural" theology that Euthyphro appeals. He enters the discussion with an integral vision which allows him to see clearly (being a seer), even to the prosecution of his father and the defense of a "heretic." At the beginning, all things are united for him: what is lovely is loved by the gods, holiness and justice are one, and service and piety the same thing. But this integral vision is not able to stand up to the analysis of Socrates's wisdom, since the idea of analysis had never before occurred to the seer and the exercise was unfamiliar. Still, he might have stood his ground. Socrates's interlocutors are usually very compliant, and Euthyphro more than most. But he might have asked Socrates if analysis is the proper way to know persons, and especially divine ones. He might even have asked the philosopher for his counter proposal, but this Socrates forestalls by playing the "disciple."

Euthyphro discerns that the gods are in some way the exemplars of virtue, a thesis no Christian would deny. But Euthyphro cannot define the way in which the warring gods exemplify; a Christian would locate his failure in following the wrong gods, or rather in following gods instead of God, and especially in following gods who lie and make war and love with equal abandon. However, the Christian ought not to be too superior on this point, since the God of Abraham is not above deceit in guiding his people, as Ahab and Jeremiah discover (cf., Jer 4:10, 20:7; Ezek 14:19; 2 Chron 18:18–22). And likewise, He is capable of hardening men's hearts, which is a way of hiding the truth from them. He also, like his pagan "colleagues," leads armies in battle and sternly orders the destruction of cities and peoples. Indeed, the only vice denied the God of the Hebrews seems to be sexual exploits, but this may merely be one of the drawbacks of being a unitarian divinity: there's no one to fool around with. The later prophets and the Christians will correct this deficiency by imposing a rich sexual imagery on the love between God and his people. Of course, the modern reader is likely to interpret all of these passages out of existence, but for the ancients, they express the truly rich and paradoxical relationship of God and man. Hesiod must therefore be confronted head-on. Euthyphro, absent the doubts raised by Socrates, is content to let the complexity of the world extend even to the heavens.

Euthyphro comes very close to the truth which is at the heart of all truths when he identifies justice with service to both gods and men. Replace the word "service" with the word "love," and you have all of the law and the prophets as well. But since he has allowed Socrates to divorce piety and justice, the moment passes, a moment that might have been decisive. Hence that moment will have to wait for another seer, and one more than a seer. For the moment in question, the seer is driven off the stage, and faith and reason go their separate ways. The wisdom of Euthyphro consists in this: an integral view of the cosmos based on a faith in divine persons as they appear in the sacred literature. This is remarkably similar to the Christian faith (or indeed, to any faith) and if it is not wise for Euthyphro, then neither can it be wise for us. This "wisdom" is, I believe, the "absurdity" to which St. Paul refers when he speaks of "shaming the wise" (1 Cor 1:27). It is not a denial of human wisdom *per se*, but rather the recognition that such wisdom by itself is not complete. Instead, it takes the "absurdities" that are common to all men, the absurdities of prayer, ritual, sacrifice, and poetry—the absurdity of faith—to complete the work of reason.

Faith and Reason

Can we therefore dispense with the wisdom of Socrates? We certainly cannot. For whatever else may be said, the sage does bring the seer to the knowledge of his own inadequacies, which is the most important knowledge in the world. Euthyphro's initial confidence is broken when the metaphysical ground beneath him shifts from radical faith to radical doubt. One by one, his assumptions are broken, until he is left with no place to stand. Hence, he must leave. And this must be the course of paganism; its *mythos* must always be at war with its *logos*; one must "win" and the other "lose"; one must stay, and the other go. And if one does not refuse to go, as Socrates refused, he must be killed.

Does Christianity escape this conundrum? Yes and no. Yes it does, because the true *Logos* is already united to its "myth"; the account comes to us not, in the first instance, as a received doctrine, but as a story told and re-told as an always new yet firm tradition, always repeated liturgically and embodied socially. All possible disputes between *mythos* and *logos*, between Hesiod and Aristotle, have already been resolved in the person and life of Jesus, the true *Logos*. But while they have been resolved in the life of Christ, they have not yet been resolved in our understanding of that life, a process which takes place only within history. The kingdom, which is already begun, is not yet realized in the world, and within that temporal field, we must still struggle, and struggle mainly with our own failure to both comprehend and actualize the Word in the world.

Because all the conundrums have *already* been resolved, in fact if not in understanding, then Christianity can expose itself to philosophy in a way that is impossible for paganism. Christianity may do so in perfect confidence that however much she may for a moment stumble, she will not fall. She will neither have to flee the court nor kill the sage. Sage and seer may find themselves at odds, but at base they will always turn out to be the best of friends. But for all that, the seer must be the elder, and the sage the student; theology must maintain her preeminence over philosophy, even while she cannot ignore the questions of her sometimes subversive subject. Only in this way can her intellectual tradition advance towards its final consummation. Theology is the queen of the sciences, and this she must remain; but she is a queen-*mother* rather than a tyrant; she listens to her subjects with care, even as she keeps her own counsel.

Jesus Christ says something rather remarkable about this subject: He claims to be "the Way, the Truth, and the Life" (John 14:6). This means that the truth is, ultimately, not some *object*, such as a pure and distinct idea, but a *subject*, an acting, self-aware person. And persons are known in a way that is fundamentally different from objects. Persons are known in love through faith, hope, and trust. It is equally true that our knowledge of the divine persons is mediated through all of the objects which are known as "creation," objects which may be known through analysis and all the techniques of science and philosophy. Thus, our knowledge of the world and the world's creator comes from two sources: objectively through the objects in the world and subjectively through faith in the creator.

Philosophy claims a preeminence over the world of objects and ideas about objects, and this claim cannot be denied.

Anyone who would study the world must, whether he realizes it or not, study some philosophy and begin with some principles. He may or may not be aware of these principles, but they are always there. But philosophy, by itself, can never be sufficient, for the world of objects does not exhaust the totality of being; indeed, it does not even exhaust the being of the philosopher. Ultimately, being resides in the divine persons, and these persons can only be known in faith and love.

When the philosophers derive their god, they tend to derive an abstraction. This abstraction, no matter how true and logical, can never be loved because, properly speaking, only persons can love and be loved. Thus, the god of the philosophers engenders no myth, has no prayer, no liturgy, and no ritual. But these are precisely the way that man relates to God, a God that is some*body* rather than some*thing*.

Letter 1

I was pleased to see your article about Plato's dialogue *Euthy-phro*, a dialogue with the typical charm of Socrates's person-ality, along with the discomfiture of his interlocutor, so typical especially of the early dialogues. Euthyphro's quick exit at the end of conversation, when called upon by Socrates to begin their discussion anew—"Another time, then, Socrates, for I am in a hurry, and must be off this minute"—is amusing after the naive and overconfident assertions he made at the beginning of the dialogue. For centuries, I would wager, that dialogue has been read and taught as an example of the triumph of philosophic wisdom over brash and untu-tored ignorance. But your article is entitled, "An Apology for Euthyphro"! How can that be? How do you defend Euthy-phro's confused reliance on myths told by poets over against Socrates's philosophical critique?

Your argument can be stated in its essence somewhat as follows, it seems to me. Socrates defeats, or appears to defeat, Euthyphro because Euthyphro's crude sort of theol-ogy is based on nothing more than poets such as Homer or Hesiod. But in fact Socrates's method of using philosophy to *analyze* (your word—about which more later) theological concepts is limited because it ends, at best, in the rather ster-ile notion of a Supreme Being or First Mover, a concept that rarely excites religious fervor. But such concepts are pretty much all that philosophy, when it turns its attention to the question of the divine—what we call natural theology—has ever claimed to arrive at. So the tradition of Socrates, even though adopted by so many Christian thinkers, doesn't seem to correspond to the real religious convictions or needs of humanity.

But there is another way, you aver. Namely the fact that

> all peoples believe certain things about the divine, among which are that the divinity is reached by prayer, ritual, and sacrifice, and that it is spoken of primarily through poetry and metaphor. . . . For there seems to be no chain of reasoning, starting with any arbitrary "first principles" you like, that ends in the conclusion, "and then you place a lamb on the altar and kill it." Indeed, the "rational" mind has a great deal of difficulty connecting the dead lamb to the living God, and yet that is what all peoples do, or something very like it.

And of course, you are right—at least to a point. Long ago Chesterton said as much in *Orthodoxy*: "Almost every great religion on earth works with the same external methods, with priests, scriptures, altars, sworn brotherhoods, special feasts." Nor do I deny, rather the contrary, that the sacrifices and myths of pagans did in many ways foreshadow the truths of the Gospel, and that these sacrifices and myths appear to be based on certain deep religious convictions of nearly all humanity, convictions that have usually not been arrived at through a process of reasoning. But despite this, I don't think I can agree with you entirely. You write:

> The wisdom of Euthyphro consists in this: an integral view of the cosmos based on a faith in divine persons as they appear in the sacred literature. This is remarkably similar to the Christian faith . . . and if it is not wise for Euthyphro, then neither can it be wise for us. This "wisdom" is, I believe, the "absurdity" to which St. Paul

refers when he speaks of "shaming the wise." It is not a denial of human wisdom *per se*, but rather the recognition that such wisdom by itself is not complete. Instead, it takes the "absurdities" that are common to all men, the absurdities of prayer, ritual, sacrifice, and poetry—the absurdity of faith—to complete the work of reason.

Granted, the Unmoved Mover God of the philosophers is in need of being filled out, as it were. But by what? By "the 'absurdities' that are common to all men, the absurdities of prayer, ritual, sacrifice, and poetry," or by revelation? In other words, despite the similarities between pagan rites and those of the Church, and despite the omnipresence of a religious instinct, are we really talking about the same thing here?

Paganism could never appeal to a historical revelation in support of itself. It depends upon stories handed down based upon nothing more than an appeal to "what was told us by our fathers." Whether that of the classical Mediterranean world or of India or anywhere else, it offered nothing but a mass of discordant stories about the divine beings, who often behaved in ways that the pagans themselves recognized as worthy of censure. Anyone with a philosophic bent, if he did not turn from such a religion with disgust, at least sought to reinterpret it fundamentally, for example, as a series of allegories. None of them could appeal to a definite revelation of the Divine, unlike the so-called Abrahamic religions, which all claim a definite historical revelation, whether truly as in Judaism and Catholicism, or falsely as in Islam, of God acting in and revealing himself in history. They are not based on myths, on timeless stories that took place no one knows when or where. Whatever theological problems remained or remain to be worked out, their foundation in historical truth could be pointed out in a way that could satisfy the criticisms of the philosopher. You and I, it would appear, are at least in principle agreed on this point, that the Faith is hardly the same as paganism, and the Faith need not fear philosophy.

Where then do we disagree? You claim a similarity between the human instinct for religion, which is what paganism ultimately rests upon, and the faith of a Christian. "The wisdom of Euthyphro consists in this: an integral view of the cosmos based on a faith in divine persons as they appear in the sacred literature. This is remarkably similar to the Christian faith . . . and if it is not wise for Euthyphro, then neither can it be wise for us." But in Sacred Scripture itself, in the first chapter of Romans, it is affirmed that God can be known not because of sacred stories or myths handed down, but through knowledge of his created works, the very method generally used by the most "rationalist" of philosophers or theologians, and proclaimed as a dogma at the First Vatican Council (Canon I, of Revelation). The presence of sacrifices and myths which in many cases have obvious analogs with the Faith does not mean that Christian belief rests on foundations in any way similar to those of pagan beliefs.

You also make much of the fact that in contrast to the near universal agreement of cultures throughout the world on the necessity of sacrifices, rites, purifications, and so on, the method of natural theology, the application of philosophy to religious questions, has never brought about much agreement, even on the part of philosophers themselves. "But it is the philosophers who can't seem to agree, while the mass of men is united on these very points." Yes, sadly true. The weaknesses and imperfections of human reasoning are all too obvious when we look at the often sharp disagreements among philosophers. You admit yourself, however, that it is not the fault of the arguments themselves. "That these ideas flow irresistibly from the logic is undeniable," you write. These disagreements must be put down to the contentiousness, pride, and the intellectual and even moral weakness that philosophers share with the rest of humanity.

And is it certain that the general agreement of mankind on many of what Chesterton called "the same external methods" means that this religious "knowledge" had nothing whatsoever to do with the sort of philosophy that Socrates practiced? When St. Paul speaks (as I mentioned above) of the fact that "what may be known about God is manifest to [the gentiles]. . . . For since the creation of the world his invisible attributes are clearly seen—his everlasting power also and divinity—being understood through the things that are made" (Romans 1:19–20), was Paul claiming that all men are capable of philosophic reasoning of the sort that Socrates engaged in? That Euthyphro, then, was truly an odd exception among a race of philosophers? Not exactly. He was claiming, I think, a sort of pre-philosophical, but by no means irrational or simply traditional knowledge of God on the part of all humanity, namely the knowledge that comes from the simple insight that if I exist, if all the things that I see around me exist, then surely all these things, always coming into being and then perishing, have been created by some Power beyond or above mere created things. This sort of reasoning, hardly expressed with the precision of St. Thomas's Five Ways, is still in a profound sense philosophic. It depends on a perfectly valid inference, even if those who half consciously made it were ignorant of the forms of Aristotle's logic.

The fact that pagans, like Christians, generally had purifying rites and initiations, altars, sacrifices, all the externals of religion, witnesses indeed to a deep recognition on the part of mankind not just of the existence of the divine, but of our dependence upon such Being or beings. Hence the inchoate desire to worship, to placate, to supplicate, whatever numinous forces might exist. But this sense of dependence upon the divine, these external similarities themselves do not, as I see it, suggest a *method* of knowing divine truths with any certainty. As Chesterton said elsewhere (in *The Everlasting Man*):

> A man did not stand up and say "I believe in Jupiter and Juno and Neptune," etc., as he stands up and says "I believe in God the Father Almighty" and the rest of the Apostles' Creed. . . . Certainly the pagan does not disbelieve like an atheist, any more than he believes like a Christian. He feels the presence of powers about which he guesses and invents. St. Paul said that the Greeks had one altar to an unknown god. But in truth all their gods were unknown gods. And the real break in history did come when St. Paul declared to them whom they had ignorantly worshipped.

The concrete facts of the Christian revelation cannot be demonstrated by philosophy, it is true, but neither are they simply guessed about or invented or accepted simply by a blind faith handed down from our ancestors.

If this is so, how then are the particular truths of the Faith to be rendered reasonable, the truths of "prayer, ritual, and sacrifice" which you mentioned earlier, as these are practiced by Christians and contained in the Church's deposit of faith? When St. Paul is speaking to the Athenian philosophical pagans in Athens, he first appeals to their knowledge of God as contained in their own writings, but proceeds to the proclamation of his new teachings, that God "has fixed a day on which he will judge the world with justice by a Man whom

he has appointed, and whom he has guaranteed to all by raising him from the dead" (Acts 17:31). This is the way in which
the unique facts claimed by revealed religion can be justified,
through an appeal to miracles, such as the Resurrection, by
which God has validated its claims. This is not an appeal to
a story, as we normally use that term, still less to myth, but
to historical claims which stand or fall with their truth or
lack thereof. This is why Paul elsewhere (1 Corinthians 15)
recounts the witnesses to the Resurrection, including the
"more than five hundred brethren . . . many of whom are
with us still. . . ." And why the First Vatican Council con-
demns those who affirm that "the divine origin of Christianity is not rightly proved" by miracles (Canon IV, of Faith).

It is a truism among Catholics that philosophy is subordinate to revealed truth. If a philosopher should assert anything
contrary to what the Church recognizes as divinely revealed,
then he has made an error in his reasoning, for revelation
stands as an external check upon the work of the philosopher. While I fully accept this, I submit that there *is* a sense in
which philosophy must judge religion. For as Socrates used
philosophy to critique Euthyphro's poetical or mythic assertions, a religion that cannot justify itself reasonably cannot
claim our rational allegiance. This is why in Holy Scripture
(1 Peter 3:15) we are exhorted, "Be ready always with an
answer to everyone who asks a reason for the hope that is in
you," and the word translated as reason is none other than
logos, meaning reason or rational account, in fact the wisdom
which Socrates sought after. As I noted above, this does not
mean that the revealed truths of the Faith can be proven by
philosophy, but it does mean that the act of faith must be reasonable, as the First Vatican Council teaches.

One more matter, about which it is not clear to me at this

point whether our differences are more semantic than substantive. You speak over and over again of philosophy as *analysis*, as "continually dividing things until their indivisible elements are reached"—a process that suggests to me physics, not metaphysics. Certainly some philosophers have worked that way, but hardly all, and the philosophical tradition stemming ultimately from Socrates, of which Aristotle and St. Thomas are the greatest representatives, does not do so. This tradition is interested in finding *wholes*, and understands that the essences of things are not discovered by division, at least not in the end, but by seeing something for what it is. Socrates is trying to strip away the accidents in order to discover essences. You describe it well when you characterize it as a "search for the essence of the good, apart from its shifting expression in the world of 'things'." What does it mean to call an apple pie good, a horse good, a man good, God good? What, if anything, does *good* mean in itself? To discover that is Socrates's project. It is not actually a project of analysis in the sense of taking apart, but of finding wholes. It is the difference between algebra and the geometry of Euclid. Both are equally mathematical, equally rigorous, but the former works by pulling apart, the latter by seeing the deepest properties and relations of wholes. But perhaps you are using *analyze* loosely, and our differences are more a matter of words than of substance.

I hope, John, that I haven't seriously read you wrongly, and I look forward to more fruitful conversation between us.

Thomas

REFERENCES

G. K. Chesterton, *The Everlasting Man*, part 1, chapter 5.
G. K. Chesterton, *Orthodoxy*, chapter 8.

Letter 2

Morning and Evening, the First Day

Dear Thomas,

First of all, thank you for your kind words and careful reading of my rather modest meditations on the *Euthyphro*. Nothing flatters a writer more than having a careful reader. And you certainly are able to point to weaknesses or at least points which require clarification. But that being said, I think your critique rests on a false choice. You say:

> Granted, the Unmoved Mover God of the philosophers is in need of being filled out, as it were. But by what? By "the 'absurdities' that are common to all men, the absurdities of prayer, ritual, sacrifice, and poetry," or by revelation? In other words, despite the similarities between pagan rites and those of the Church, and despite the omnipresence of a religious instinct, are we really talking about the same thing here?

Here, it seems to me, you place a quarrel between "prayer, ritual, sacrifice, poetry" and "revelation." But what is that revelation, except for a collection of prayers, rituals, and stories? The psalm, the story, and the sermon are what convey the revelation, which is then commemorated by the ritual. Hence, if that choice were the difference, there would be no difference at all. The story leads us to the revelation, but the revelation points us back to the story. This cannot be where the difference between us and pagans lies.

I take it that we would agree that Jesus gives us the best gifts possible. Should we not then agree that the poetry is a better gift than the philosophy? Jesus Christ refuses to give us a "doctrine"; rather he gives us a biography. Or more precisely, he gives us his life and his disciples give us his biography, or rather four of them, each of which differs from the others in important ways. He interprets the prophecies of the Jews not in a dissertation, but by being himself and in his own life that interpretation. He gives us a Sermon on the Mount, not a Seminar in the Synagogue; he gives us miracles, not propositions. He gives us his very life, and leaves the interpretation to his church. Indeed, the major doctrines of Christianity—say, the hypostatic union and the Trinity—are nowhere mentioned in the Scriptures. Even the Incarnation, the defining tenet of Christianity, is not clearly stated and is given in terms which will bear any number of plausible interpretations. Indeed, it took three or four centuries to work these things out with any degree of precision. Assuming of course that they can be (or should be) defined precisely, because for that work twenty centuries have not been enough.

You also offer as a difference the claim that the pagans "offered nothing but a mass of discordant stories about the divine beings, who often behaved in ways that the pagans themselves recognized as worthy of censure." But surely this is equally true of YWHW, the God of the Hebrews who is also our God. Surely, the slaughters of Joshua are more than enough to satisfy the blood lust of the most avaricious of the pagan gods. And as for "discordant" stories, surely much of the Old Testament is of dubious historical value (including

the aforementioned *Joshua*) and the Gospels themselves cannot be precisely correlated. So the difference must lie elsewhere.

You also offer miracles as final proof, but this is dangerous
ground. For without belaboring the point too much, I can
point out that every religion makes this claim. If that's the
difference, it's just a dispute about who can make the more
fantastic claims, and then there is no real difference because
there is no way to arbitrate the claims. It is worth reflecting
on this, the fortieth anniversary of the Jim Jones massacre,
that Jones's services were full of people testifying to the miracles Jones had wrought among them. Miracles do "prove"
the faith, but not in the sense you seem to mean that (correct
me if I am misreading you); our philosophical claims are not,
and cannot be, validated by miracles.

It is perplexing that you attribute the failure of the philosophers to come to any agreement among themselves to "the
contentiousness, pride, and the intellectual and even moral
weakness that philosophers share with the rest of humanity"
and not to the insufficiency of reason as such to reach the
divine. But is this not to have your cake and eat it too? For
reason is always exercised by persons who share these char-
acteristics, and share them whether they are Christian or no.
Hence, even if abstract reason were capable of reaching the
truth of God, *our* reason is not. If you are claiming that there
exists a "right reason" in some abstract realm, well and good,
but that is no guarantee that we can reach it, and even less
assurance that our faith corrects the faults of reason, given
that even the Christian philosophers cannot reach agreement. Should we be more concerned with the *quiddity* of
things along with Aquinas, or with their *haecceity* along with
Scotus? The Faith seems indifferent to our answers, and the

contending sages are, respectively, hailed as the Angelic Doctor and the Subtle Doctor.

You cite the first chapter of Romans to support your view, but it seems to me that Greek "wisdom" is precisely what Paul is attacking, because the Greeks became "vain in their reasoning and their senseless minds were darkened" (Romans 1:21). Hence, "While claiming to be wise, they became fools" (22). Paul actually addresses this specifically in 1 Corinthians:

> For it is written: "I will destroy the wisdom of the wise, and the learning of the learned I will set aside." Where is the wise one? Where is the scribe? Where is the debater of this age? Has not God made the wisdom of the world foolish? For since in the wisdom of God the world did not come to know God through wisdom, it was the will of God through the foolishness of the proclamation to save those who have faith. For Jews demand signs and Greeks look for wisdom, but we proclaim Christ crucified, a stumbling block to Jews and foolishness to Gentiles, but to those who are called, Jews and Greeks alike, Christ the power of God and the wisdom of God. For the foolishness of God is wiser than human wisdom, and the weakness of God is stronger than human strength. (1 Cor 1:19–25)

Should we not think this applies equally to our own "wisdom"? Are we exempt from this law? I think not, and I am sure that I am not. This is not humility on my part; I claim a certain amount of wisdom, but I am not such a fool as to overweight that wisdom, or allow it to confine or define my faith (weak as that is).

You correctly cite 1 Peter 3:15, but I read the Greek differently. Peter's advice is given to those who are asked by the pagans for a λόγον ("logos" in Greek = *reason*), but what

Peter tells them to give is an ἀπολογίαν (*apology*), "a speech in defense" of something. This is a term from rhetoric, and such speeches would include not only arguments from "logos" (logic) but also from "ethos" (ethics) and "pathos" (emotion). He is not telling them to become philosophers, but apologists. No doubt philosophy may be included in such an apology, but the apology is not a work of philosophy. And further, it is hope that is prior in Peter, and of course this hope, along with love, is what makes up the faith.

Finally, you say that I interpret philosophy as analysis, a continual dividing of things into their parts, whereas Thomas Aquinas is not seeking analysis, but integrals, wholes. But that is not the method of Thomas. Thomas relies on the *dialectic*. He divides everything into discrete questions, divides the questions into parts which presumably exhaust the question, and for each part applies a dialectical method to reach a "secure" answer. Now, I am sure that there are certain problems which yield to a dialectic. But I am just as certain that dialectic is not and cannot be the primary method of theology. Such rationalism, while it represents a bridge to the modern world, also represented a break with older methods of doing theology. There was a good reason that the introduction of Aristotelianism was always controversial and frequently condemned. And however one decides that controversy, I will assert that Thomas is more implicated in modernity than the Scholastics are willing to admit. It is impossible for a dialectical theology to avoid the risk of mere rationalism; there is a direct line from Aquinas to Descartes.

I hope all of that gives some apology for the points that you raise. But now I turn to the point on which we are agreed, although I suspect we understand it in different ways. You said:

None of them could appeal to a definite revelation of
the Divine, unlike the so-called Abrahamic religions,
which all claim a definite historical revelation, whether
truly as in Judaism and Catholicism, or falsely as in
Islam, of God acting in and revealing himself in history.
They are not based on myths, on timeless stories that
took place no one knows when or where.

This, the purely historical unfolding of revelation, is where
the difference between Christianity and all the other religions lies. But the interpretation of this difference depends
on how we understand the terms "history" and "myth."

It is not correct to say that the pagans did not know "when
or where" these myths took place. Indeed, they knew precisely when and where, as these were the only things they did
know precisely. They took place in *mythic* time and in the
ethereal realms. Mythic time for the pagans is real time; what
we call "real time"—history—was ephemeral and unreliable.
Moreover, historical time was cyclic, just an endless cycle of
decay from a foundational "golden age" to the present corrupt moment, which would inevitably end in collapse and be
succeeded by a new golden age when the cycle would begin
again. Nothing cosmically important happens in history; it is
just an endless descent into folly. All important things happen
in mythic time and have already happened. Quite literally,
there is no future.

Modern parlance equates "myth" with "lie"; the ancients
equated it with truth, and the only kind of truth that
endured. The rituals of the pagans reenact the events of their
"real time" to give historical time some sense of permanence. For example, when the Romans founded a city, they
first performed the rituals connected with the myth of the
founding of the world, because each city was itself a micro-

cosm, a "little cosmos." The rituals inject the *mythos* into the *cosmos*, thereby prolonging its life. Furthermore—and here is the important point—the history could not really be known. The kings might record their mighty deeds, and some might actually believe them, but for the most part the past was past and the future was bleak. Only the myth was real. This explains the general pagan indifference to historical studies.

Nor are the pagans entirely wrong: you cannot recover the past. It is gone, and available only in records, monuments, artifacts, and traditions. The modern world would have us believe that history is a science through which we can grasp the past with great certainty, but this is dubious. What happens is that the historian takes the fragments and assembles them into a story about the past. Or rather stories, because different historians tell different stories, each of which embodies a different understanding. For example, we can know with precision when the Civil War began, but we can only argue about why it began. North and South tell a different story, and for each the history, the story they tell, enters into the realm of myth, a "truth" that endures, a "truth" that is their founding story, their enduring myth. Note that myth and history change places: history first, and then myth, albeit competing myths.

We can thank the Jews for this priority of history over myth. The Jews in exile come into contact with the pagan myth of the *Enuma Elish* and rework it into their own myth in Genesis 1. And their major contribution comes in one single line: "Morning and evening, the first day." Creation was *in time*, historical time. Myth moves from the ethereal realm and into human history. Surely, the pagans laughed at them: "There is no Sun or Moon, but you insist on morning and evening?" To which the Hebrew will only reply, "Morning and evening, the first day." His faith in history is unshakable, even when it is illogical. It is not important to argue whether the six days actually happened as recorded; it is only necessary to know that from that moment on, it is time—history—which will give shape to the formless void and give meaning to the life of man. The revelation of God is in history and through history. The revelation will be carried on by real men in real time. Even if the stories are legendary, they are nonetheless historical, or assumed to be so.

But the Jewish story has a problem. The Jews are the first progressives: history starts some time and goes somewhere. But where, they could not precisely say. In exile, they picked up stories of resurrection and a final battle between good and evil, but these elements sort of hang in the air and are never precisely resolved, at least not at the time of Christ. One portion of Judaism rejects and another accepts this final consummation of history. And the story remains tribal, peculiar to the Jews and mainly concerned with their own destiny.

It remained for the Christian story to give a definite shape to history and to turn it from a tribal to a universal story. For when the Christian God injects himself into history, being born into a particular time and place, history reaches its climactic point. Here was something really new, something that changed everything. From there, history proceeds inevitably towards its *dénouement*. Now we have a real story, and a story with real actors, namely ourselves. Yes, we know, in some vague sense, how the story ends. But how it gets there is always a mystery; we must live the story, must become actors in the "theo-drama" of history (as Hans Urs von Balthasar names it) as the story of salvation unfolds itself in our own stories. This is crucial. For the pagans, individual histories had no impact on the myth. But in Christianity, we are myth; our histories advance the story towards its final end.

Jesus Christ unites the *mythos* and the *logos* in his own person and his own history. He brings the enduring truth, which is himself, and injects it into human time, which becomes our history. And since the history is an interpretation of the past, it is not necessary that it be correct in all its details. It is not really necessary to harmonize the Gospels, any more than it is necessary to believe that the world was created in 144 hours. What is necessary to believe is that the world is created in time, that God reveals himself progressively through history, and that he personally enters that history as its climax and redeemer.

What is primary here is the story. And this is why we are given a story and not a philosophy. True, we must constantly reflect on that story; some of this reflection will be philosophical, some mystical, some artistic, but mostly it will be a reflection in action, in *doing* the will of the Father. And crucial to acting is reenacting the story, which is liturgy. Which is to say it is prayer, poetry, sermon, and sacrifice. So the proper order is this: poetry first; philosophy later, but philosophy *only* to better penetrate the poetry; we leave the poetry only to be able to return to it. Like Chesterton's pilgrim, we leave our home and travel around the world, only to return—and rediscover—our home, and discover it as something fresh and new.

But I must close with a question: Why are you trying to render the story reasonable? Why rationalize the absurdities? It is absurd that water becomes wine, wine becomes blood, and that God becomes man, suffering a horrible death so that man can become like God. And it is the most absurd thing of all that a man should rise from the dead. I have no desire to rationalize these things. To do so would be to bind God with chains of logic, and so make the whole story necessary rather than free. But it is free precisely because it is irrational; it does not spring from reason, but from love, and love transcends all reason. Hence, we may say, *credo quia absurdum*, because love is always absurd.

John

Letter 3

DEAR JOHN,

Thank you for your careful consideration of my response to your *Euthyphro* article. In these days of tweets and combox insults, such cordial intellectual engagement is indeed welcome! But I still find myself unable to agree with you, as you will see.

I posited a distinction between, or placed "a quarrel between," as you put it, the myths and sacred stories of pagans, handed down without being rooted in any historical revelation, and revelation as we find it in the life and teaching of Jesus Christ. "But," you say, "what is revelation, except for a collection of prayers, rituals, and stories?" If you mean by this that we possess a collection of stories about a personage, one Jesus, which contains frequent prayers and some rituals, yes, this is certainly true. Is this, however, the primary locus of God's revelation of the New Covenant? Just before his Ascension, Christ told his apostles, "Go therefore and make disciples of all nations . . , teaching them to observe all that I have commanded you..." (Matt 28:19–20). *This* is what the Church's earliest evangelists communicated. If we consider both the apostolic preaching as recorded in Acts, and the life of the New Testament Church so far as that is reflected in the epistles of the New Testament, there is little interest in the details of the life of Christ, except for the great saving mysteries of his death and Resurrection. As C. S. Lewis's devil, Screwtape, put it,

> No nation, and few individuals, are really brought into the Enemy's camp by the historical study of the biography of Jesus, simply as biography. Indeed materials for a full biography have been withheld from men. The earliest converts were converted by a single historical fact (the Resurrection) and a single theological doctrine (the Redemption) operating on a sense of sin which they already had. . . .

Still less were conversions effected from a preaching or reading of the Old Testament narratives. Obviously those narratives could not be repudiated, for Christ's status as Messiah of the Jews depends upon the historical tradition of Israel. But beyond that, beyond affirming that the Church was the new Israel and somehow both inherited and transformed the mission of the old Israel, she has defined little about the various and sundry books of the old law, either as to their teaching or their precise historical character, and indeed in her liturgy makes rather free use of their contents and imagery for her own purposes.

Are you not confusing a certain outward resemblance between, say, the Gospel stories or even the Old Testament narratives, and the tales of the pagan poets? It is true that no serious critic would claim absolute historicity, as we use that term today, for all of what are called the historical books of the Old Testament, and certainly some of them were hardly meant to be understood as such. But just because they contain "prayers, rituals, and stories" does not mean that they can be equated with similar literary productions of pagans.

Since I have mentioned the Resurrection, this might be the place to talk about miracles. "You also offer miracles as final proof, but this is dangerous ground. For . . . I can point out that every religion makes this claim." Yes, I suppose that every religion, or nearly so, has such stories. Whether they assert them as a claim for the credibility of their teachings is another matter, which there is no need to go into. But the real point here, it seems to me, is that from the beginning the apostolic preaching *did* base its claims upon miracles, especially the miracle of the Resurrection of Jesus Christ: "if Christ has not been raised, then our preaching is in vain and your faith is in vain" (1 Cor 15:14). The apostles and their companions made this claim because they believed it to be true, fully aware of the multitude of marvelous stories told by pagans. And I am not prepared to assert that God has *never*, in the immense benignity of his love, answered the prayer of a pagan, even perhaps to the extent of performing of a miracle. But this is not the point, because such miraculous interventions, if they ever occurred, did not occur in attestation of some divine truth. And the Church claims such miracles, and continues to do so, precisely in attestation of her divine truths. Yes, probably all religions make claims to miracles of some kind. The apostles doubtless knew that. But this did not deter them from making *their* claims to the miraculous, and making the further claim that they could verify the miracles, as in Paul's recounting of the witnesses to the Resurrection in 1 Corinthians 15. No, to bring up miracles is not to tread upon "dangerous ground," as you argue, for the Church has never hesitated to bring up miracles, and to offer human testimony and other kinds of proof for them. I know there are some who look upon this kind of activity, for example, the Medical Bureau at Lourdes, as unfortunate relics of nineteenth-century rationalism, but it seems to me they are simply a continuation of the same approach taken by the apostles: to use well-attested miracles as part of our apologetic.

But to return to the main question. Religion, which claims in part at least to communicate knowledge of things divine, of man's fate after death and so on, has only one source whence to draw such knowledge: from God or from some accredited messenger of God. When the historical record opens for us, we find the world's religious life dominated by what we call paganism. Certainly there are varieties of paganisms, but all these varieties have one thing in common. They are based solely on sacred stories that have been handed down from those who went before. But such stories cannot claim any warrant for their truth. Their only claim to belief is that "this is what our fathers told us." Hence the necessary attitude of paganism toward the content of its own religious traditions is illustrated well by this narrative from Book II of St. Bede's *Ecclesiastical History*. After St. Paulinus had presented the Gospel to the King of Northumbria, the King asked his royal counselors for their advice. One of them spoke as follows:

> The present life of man, O king, seems to me, in comparison of that time which is unknown to us, like to the swift flight of a sparrow through the room wherein you sit at supper in winter, with your commanders and ministers, and a good fire in the midst, whilst the storms of rain and snow prevail abroad; the sparrow, I say, flying in at one door, and immediately out at another, whilst he is within, is safe from the wintry storm; but after a short space of fair weather, he immediately vanishes out of your sight, into the dark winter from which he had emerged. So this life of man appears for a short space, but of what went before, or what is to follow, we are utterly ignorant. If, therefore, this

new doctrine contains something more certain, it seems justly to deserve to be followed.

It is this "something more certain" claimed by the "new doctrine" that is the note which distinguishes from paganism a religion that claims a basis in an historic revelation. God has spoken, and spoken not at some undetermined time in the past to unknown persons, but spoken to some real flesh and blood human being, someone who can be identified as the receiver of God's revelation, and whose credentials can therefore be evaluated.

Now I made this point already when I said that paganism could not "appeal to a definite revelation of the Divine, unlike the so-called Abrahamic religions, which all claim a definite historical revelation . . . not based on myths, timeless stories that took place no one knows when or where." To which you make two responses. One is that I draw too sharp a distinction between Christians and pagans, for, you say, "what is revelation, except for a collection of prayers, rituals, and stories? . . . This cannot be where the difference between us and pagans lies." I responded to this point above already.

But you make a second charge, I think, that is more serious. You write:

> It is not correct to say that the pagans did not know "when or where" these myths took place. Indeed, they knew precisely when and where, as these were the only things they did know precisely. They took place in *mythic* time and in the *ethereal* realms. Mythic time for the pagans is real time; what we call "real time"—history—was ephemeral and unreliable. Moreover, historical time was cyclic, just an endless cycle of decay from a foundational "golden age" to the present corrupt moment. . . .

45

Certainly the concept of history as cyclical is a commonplace of paganism. But is it quite so clear that there was *no* notion of or interest in history—not, certainly, with all the contemporary refinements of scholarship (which were largely missing even as late as eighteenth-century historians such as Gibbon), but with a recognition that the events of human life and history did unfold in some manner, even if all that was would eventually be destroyed and renewed? The Greeks dated things by the Olympiads, the Romans from the presumed date of the founding of their city. Indeed, the earliest Greek poetry we possess is not Hesiod, with his genealogies of the gods, but Homer, writing about the Trojan war, a real event, considerably embellished and fancifully related, it is true, but based on something that actually happened in this world. When we come to later times, this is even more obvious. Herodotus evidences interest not only in the recent events of the Persian invasion, but, surprisingly, makes some rather sophisticated comments about archaic Greek history, about which even now historians are less than certain. (See, for example, his discussion in Book V of the Greek adoption of the Phoenician alphabet.)

But your argument proceeds further. "Modern parlance equates 'myth' with 'lie'; the ancients equated it with truth, and the only kind of truth that endured." Whatever the archaic mentality might have been, the pagans, in the records left to us, were perfectly able to distinguish myth from history, fable from fact. Cicero, for example, offers critiques of mythic claims, as when in his *De legibus* he debunks the claim that certain relics from the times of Homer, shown to visitors to Athens, were really what they were claimed to be. In another work (*De re publica*) he refers to the proclivity of men from more rustic ages to invent and believe stories, such as human beings becoming gods, and in the same work recounts a Róman officer explaining to his troops that the sudden darkening of the moon was not a supernatural event (*prodigium*), but resulted from the sun's light being blocked from reaching the moon.

But what of history then? Here you very much surprise me when you write that "the pagans [were not] entirely wrong" in giving priority to stories over history.

> What happens is that the historian takes the fragments [of the past] and assembles them into a story about the past. Or rather stories, because different historians tell different stories. . . . So for example, we can know with precision when the Civil War began, but we can only argue about why it began. North and South tell a different story. . . .

One can concede that the interpretation of historical events is often less than complete and even open to more than one interpretation, but are we thereby reduced merely to telling different stories, no better than tribal tales? Surely the fact that historians of the Civil War, to use your example, appeal to the factual record indicates their desire to ground their interpretations in history. Some historians, to be sure, are more honest about this than others; some rather shamelessly fail to mention things which they presume their readers are unaware of, but that is not honest historical writing. Where there is a mass of data, different judgments of that data are certainly possible, but is this all we can say of history? Are all historical interpretations equally probable, and equally to be ascribed to mere tribal bias? If challenged, would not a Southern historian or a Northern historian appeal to facts in support of his position, rather than just say, "Well, that's *my* narrative, I'm just part of that tribe"? Do you really want to deny that in *many* cases, not all to be sure, honest historians have achieved a degree of understanding of motives, even in the midst of a complexity of events?

But it was the Jews, you assert, who did something different, whom "we can thank for [a] priority of history over myth," but, to summarize your thought—I hope not to distort it too much—they did it badly.

> The Jews are the first progressives: history starts some time and goes somewhere. But where they could not precisely say. In exile, they picked up stories of resurrection and a final battle between good and evil, but these elements sort of hang in the air and are never precisely resolved. . . . And the story remains tribal, peculiar to the Jews and mainly concerned with their own destiny.

You say, though, and I agree, that it was the Church that took this "from a tribal story to a universal story." Very true. But *story*? It is, I grant, not a theological or philosophical lecture. Perhaps I should call it primarily a *claim*, a claim (to the Jews) that "this Jesus, whom I proclaim to you, is the Christ" (Acts 17:3), and a claim (to the Gentiles) that God "has fixed a day on which he will judge the world in righteousness by a man whom he has appointed, and of this he has given assurance to all men by raising him from the dead" (Acts 17:31). This is a claim made about a unique historical event, but that does not mean it is merely a story, more or less on the level with the stories that pagans tell.

Given your earlier remarks about history and the interpretation of history as simply *story*, I am unclear as to what you mean when you discuss the events recounted in the Gospels. Are they, or is the account of the early Church in Acts, mere stories—stories that, on your account, seem to amount in

48

the end to purely subjective accounts that will differ depending upon one's point of view? It is true, as you say, that it is "not really necessary to harmonize the Gospels," but this, I would say, is because we lack a complete understanding of their exact literary forms, of the Evangelists' varying purposes in writing, of their sources and the use they made of them, and so on, not because there is some kind of necessary lack of objectivity that attaches to them and to historical accounts in general. If we had the data and the historical tools to harmonize the Gospels, I think that would be a worthwhile project indeed.

I referred to two passages of Scripture in support of my thesis that the presentation of the Faith, since New Testament times, has never been disconnected from *logos*, from a reasoned account, with all that that implies of the tradition of Greek intellectual inquiry. In the first chapter of St. Paul's epistle to the Romans, he makes the claim that has been used again and again by Christians as evidence that the existence of God is something accessible to human reason:

> what may be known about God is manifest to [the gentiles]. . . . For since the creation of the world his invisible attributes are clearly seen—his everlasting power also and divinity—being understood through the things that are made. (Rom 1:19–20)

I do not see any possible way to understand this text except as an acknowledgement that human reason can attain to some knowledge of God. Thus, whatever Paul was addressing in the passages from 1 Corinthians that you quote, about destroying "the wisdom of the wise" and so forth, is hardly to the point here. Paul's thought is not always clear (as Scripture itself notes in 2 Peter 3), and his rhetoric can be extreme, and its meaning very much depends upon the point he is addressing, which is the reason why heretics of all stripes have appealed to Paul's words to support their errors.

The other scriptural text I referenced was 1 Peter 3:15, and whether the *logos* there refers to the answer demanded or the answer to be given, the ultimate effect is the same, I think. In fact, when you write that Peter was "not telling them to become philosophers, but apologists," I do not disagree. Obviously philosophy cannot do more than demonstrate what we used to call the preambles of the Faith, but they are important preambles, nonetheless, for they render our defense something worthy of *logos*. If we did not have these preambles, and if we did not have the sorts of eye-witness testimony that Paul appealed to in support of the Resurrection, then we would be reduced to emotional appeals to make a leap of faith, just to trust, just to believe, and we would indeed merit the scorn that the New Atheists heap on what they understand as the Christian concept of faith—or reduced, perhaps, to just uttering our story, one among many stories, and thus having no more warrant for belief or acceptance than any other. All would depend upon one's personal delight in or predilection for this or that story.

You ask me, in closing, why am I "trying to render the story reasonable? Why rationalize the absurdities? It is absurd that water becomes wine, wine becomes blood, and that God becomes man. . . ." Absurd? No, I don't think so. If we perceive by means of his works the existence of the God who made all things out of nothing, then is it *absurd* that he can change water into wine or wine into blood? A *mystery*, yes, but a mystery need not be an absurdity. Unless we want to dissociate ourselves from the tradition of Greek thought, a tradition which the Church has almost always embraced, absurdities are to be shunned, not welcomed. Pope Benedict expressed it well in his Regensburg address, "nicht vernunft-gemäß, nicht 'σὺν λόγω' zu handeln, ist dem Wesen Gottes zuwider"—not to act according to reason [*logos*] is contrary to the being of God.

So I close with a question to you, in turn. How are we to render the Faith reasonable, what sort of defense are we able to make, if we shun or downplay reason, miracles, history? What in fact is left for us to do?

Thomas

REFERENCES

St. Bede, *Ecclesiastical History of the English Nation*, Book II, chapter 13.

Benedict XVI, "Meeting with the Representatives of Science, Lecture of the Holy Father," Aula Magna of the University of Regensburg, 12 September 2006.

Cicero, *De legibus*, Book I, 1.

Cicero, *De re publica*, Book I, XV.

Herodotus, *Histories*, Book V, 58–59.

C. S. Lewis, *The Screwtape Letters*, Letter XXIII.

Letter 4
Nothing but the Facts?

Dear Thomas,

I am sorry it has taken me so long to get back to you, but I was in the middle of grading term papers. I was pleased with how well my students did, with a few exceptions. But I am like that terrible boss, the one everyone has had, who takes credit for all his employees' successes but blames them for all his failures. So I take the brilliant papers as proof of my brilliant instruction, and blame the bad papers on their lack of attention. That's my story, and I'm sticking to it.

But I gather that "story" is exactly the term that most bothers you. This is evident from the descriptors with which you surround the term: "merely a story," "simply story," or simply, "*story?*" I gather that you would prefer that the faith be grounded in facts, and that we should start with the facts and then get to the faith. This is not an unreasonable attitude because it is self-evident that a story might not be true, like the story of my teaching skills. Hence your preference for facts as prior to faith. I could go along with that, if I believed in facts. But as Alasdair MacIntyre points out, "facts, like telescopes and wigs for gentlemen, were a seventeenth-century invention." MacIntyre goes on to say:

> It is of course and always was harmless, philosophically and otherwise, to use the word 'fact' of what a judgment states. What is and was not harmless, but highly

53

misleading, was to conceive of a realm of facts independent of judgment or of any other form of linguistic expression, so that judgments or statements or sentences could be paired off with facts, truth or falsity being the alleged relationship between such paired items.

I think MacIntyre is right: to call something a "fact" is to render a judgment on the existence or significance of a thing, a judgment that is always encased in a linguistic apparatus, an apparatus that is always (I will argue) part of a story.

The relationship of facts to theories is worth some reflection. Francis Bacon, considered the father of modern science, believed that we could simply gaze at the facts of nature and the truth would emerge, and man, if he could root himself in this factual gaze, would become master of all knowledge and the world would become "The Kingdom of Man." What Bacon failed to realize was that our gaze was already an act of selection, already dependent on a theory; what we see in the world is dependent on what we choose to see. What Bacon was really doing was telling a story about how nature really is. It is a story that allowed him to believe that all things could be explained by the motions of matter. For all I know this is God's own truth, but it is far from being a fact since we are far from a materialist "theory of everything." Bacon's story allowed him to see certain things as "facts" and to fashion a philosophy based on these facts. But when he failed to realize that his facts were rooted in his story, he placed his story beyond any literary analysis that could test it for truth or coherence. But we shouldn't sneer too much at Francis, since we all do the same thing.

The modern world, following Bacon, tends to see facts as prior to theories. However, the relation between theories and facts might be compared to map-making. Every map, to be useful, must exclude more of the "real world" than it includes. And what is included depends on the purpose of the map. So, for example, a road map will contain one set of "facts," a topological map another, and a political map a third. Each map will have a different set of "facts" and the rest, the "facts" of another map, will be considered irrelevant detail.

What constitutes a "fact," then, is dependent on prior choices we have made. So for example, in the mundane world of economics, we find that "facts" in fact are rooted in judgments of value. A statement like, "The unemployment rate is 3.7%" certainly looks like a "value-free fact," but as the economist Charles Clark points out, in reaching that "fact," the economist

> must first start by making the decision that it needs theoretical explanation and second [he] must define what unemployment is, both of which are blatantly value-laden (and political) activities. Furthermore, the choice of what methods to use to investigate this phenomenon also involves value judgments, as does selection of the critical criteria about what will be accepted as the "final term" in the analysis, the bases of what arguments will or will not be accepted. However, values and value judgments enter into theory construction on the ground floor by giving the theorist the "vision" of the reality s(he) is attempting to explain. This "vision" is pre-analytical in the sense that it exists before theoretical activity takes place.

I think that Clark is right to place value-judgments and beliefs prior to "facts," because the plain fact of the matter is that *theories do not arise from facts, but facts from theories.* It is the theory of the map that decides what the facts for that map are; it is the economist's theory that determines the facts of unemployment. One hopes that the theory is rooted in sound evidence (a word I prefer to "facts") but we are not really interested in the discrete phenomena that constitute the evidence, but the way the phenomena are woven together into a theory, or as I would prefer to term it, a story. We could use a variety of terms to describe this assemblage of the discrete phenomena into coherent patterns; we could call it a "theory" or an "ideology," for example. But I think "story" conveys a richer view and allows for a wider field of critique and analysis.

The preference for the term "story" requires some explanation. All the grand theories take on the structure of a narrative. The materialist tells a story that begins with a big bang and ends (I suppose) with the heat death of the cosmos. In between, matter forms stars, stars spin off planets, planets nurture life, life becomes self-conscious, etc. The theist, on the other hand, tells a story that begins with creation by a loving God and ends with a final judgment. In between is everything we know as natural and human history. In one story everything is explained, ultimately, by the motions of matter, and in the other by the will of God. Now it should be clear that one story is about as mystical as the other, since neither can explain its starting point, and both rely on things which are, as yet, beyond any real evidence. Both must be accepted or rejected *sola fide*. These grand narratives organize all the information we receive and judge what fits the narrative and what doesn't, and hence what is accepted or rejected as real evidence, as factual or non-factual. The materialist who sneers at the idea of faith does so only by ignoring his own leap of faith, and the theist who doubts the material evidence does so only by compromising his own case. But once both sides are able to grasp their theories as grand narratives, or "meta-narratives" in the current philosophical jargon, the discussion takes on a different cast. It becomes a comparison of narratives to see which has more explanatory power.

This priority of judgment over facts is crucial for our consideration of the two other issues in your letter: history and the role of miracles. To start with history, you correctly point out that ancient man was quite capable of distinguishing between history and myth. But you miss my point, which perhaps I did not make clear, that history for them was not the locus of truth. History was the locus of glory and power and grandeur and tragedy, but not the locus of truth. The eternal truths remained in the eternal realms, to be revealed in timeless stories. But the Hebrew revolution was to transfer truth and revelation to the temporal realm, to history. "Morning and evening the first day" is the first incarnation of truth in history. Creation was, from then on, in time and with time. Revelation was in time. The Way, the Truth, and the Life are now in time and with time. *This* and *this alone* distinguishes our story from that of the pagans: history acquires an ultimate religious significance.

But these histories can never be anything more than stories. In the first place, just as you cannot put everything in a map, so you could not put everything in a history. And we don't even have access to "everything," but only to such artifacts as have survived the ages and the elements. So the historian must select the elements that contribute to his story, while always bearing in mind that other stories are possible. This, I take it, is a problem for you, since there can be many conflicting accounts, such as Northern and Southern accounts of the Civil War. But I think that is less problematic, at least in theory: one merely compares the stories to see which is more comprehensive and hence has greater explanatory power. Stories that either exclude slavery as a cause or reduce all the causes to slavery will be forced to leave out many things, and the result will be incoherent. We judge the history by how many known events can be included in the analysis.

Now I think we come to the point that most divides us. We both agree that Christianity, unlike paganism, makes purely historical claims; where we differ is whether the claims can be completely referred to history. Alas, they cannot. The central mysteries—the Godhead of Jesus and the Resurrection—cannot possibly be verified by any historical method. In the case of the divinity of Jesus, the problem is obvious: there is no historical test for such a claim; it is simply beyond the competence of historians. But the Resurrection is likewise unverifiable. True, there are witnesses, but there are about as many witnesses to the risen Christ as there are to the Golden Tablets and magic spectacles of the Book of Mormon. And all the witnesses in both cases share this characteristic: they are all members of the cult. Jesus refuses to show himself to those without faith, and the Angel Moroni does the same. No historian would give credence to an event seen only by those who have an interest in that event. If Jesus had elected to show himself to Caiaphas or to Pilate, that would be one thing, but he doesn't. A prior faith in Jesus is the prerequisite to being shown the risen Jesus. *Faith* is prior to, and a prerequisite for, the acceptance of the Resurrection as history, just as today it is the prerequisite for seeing Christ in the Eucharist; the prime historical event is beyond the grasp of the historian.

With the Incarnation, the Absolutely Transcendent descends into history, but with the Resurrection and Ascension,

He rises again, taking all history with him into that realm that the ancients would call *mythic*. Christ is thus both *logos* and *mythos*; the mythic past is not jettisoned, it is baptized. The central events are historical, but not in any way reachable by the historian; they can be reached by faith alone. In this, we are in the same predicament as the pagans: we believe because our fathers, and especially the Fathers, did, and they passed it on to us. The question cannot be resolved by any human wisdom, scientific or otherwise, as Paul makes clear in the first chapter of Romans. The "sensible" historian must conclude that they hid the body, because this is a mystery not reached by the senses or by any historical methodology. By insisting on a strict "historicity," you load the dice so that Christianity can never win the game. You move the game onto Francis Bacon's ground, and on that ground Francis will beat you every time.

This marriage of *mythos* and *logos* gives Christian life a completely different cast from pagan life. The mythic elements, the elements that cannot be rationalized—prayer and liturgy—remain as central to us as they were to the pagans. But when we turn to philosophy or theology, the situation is quite different. The Greek "Enlightenment," the age of Parmenides, Socrates, Plato, and Aristotle, could advance only by rejecting, in whole or in part, the Homeric mythology. And this remained the situation right up to the time of Christ and after: the world was caught between myth and philosophy. But Christian philosophy advances by embracing its historic and mythic roots; the two are united, and neither is rejected or relativized.

This brings us to the question of miracles. Every religion, or nearly, is rooted in some foundational miracle, and every religion, or nearly, offers miracles as testimony; magic is the most common element in religion. I speak as one who has witnessed and personally benefitted from miracles, and I can say that while my faith might be strengthened by these miracles, it is not founded on them. The miracles are founded on the faith, and not the other way round. This is clear in Mark 6:5: "He was amazed at their lack of faith" and "he could perform no miracles there." I suspect that he could perform miracles there, but the faithless could not see them. Satan demands miracles; demands that the stones be turned into bread and that Jesus should hurl himself off the pinnacle of the Temple. But all Jesus will give him is Scripture. Herod wants to see a miracle, but all Jesus will give him is silence. In the synagogue, he cures the man with the withered hand, but all the Jews could see is work done on the Sabbath, because this is all their story permits them to see. And he cured all their afflictions, but the crowd still asks for Barabbas. The Jews ask for signs, but all they will get is the absurdity and stumbling block of Christ crucified. As I mentioned before, the risen Christ is shown only to those who have faith, and not because of any parsimony on God's part, but because that is the only way it can be.

So I think it stands thus: you want facts and I want faith; your faith is rooted in facts, and my facts are rooted in faith. You want miracles that you might have faith; I want faith that I might see the miracles. And this faith arises from a story. This story is a history, but it is not reachable by any historical method; it can only be accepted on faith alone. So there are no "mere stories"; there are only good and bad stories, better and worse stories. We cannot out-argue our modern pagans, we can only out-narrate them. We can only tell a better story, and we can tell this story only by living it. We don't convert the world because we don't live our story. No one

Letter 4

says any longer, "look at these Christians, how they love one another." If we did, we would convert the world, not through philosophy but through love. Reason and history are not up to the task; love alone preaches the God who is love.

Yours in Christ,
John

REFERENCES

Charles M.A. Clark, "Economic Insights from the Catholic Social Thought Tradition: Towards a More Just Economy" (2005), 6.

Alasdair MacIntyre, *Whose Justice? Which Rationality?* (Notre Dame: University of Notre Dame Press, 1988), 357–58.

Letter 5

DEAR JOHN,

Your letter so much about stories certainly chimes in with this time of the year—so close to Christmas. Why, even the most "rationalistic" of Catholics will talk about the Christmas *story*. Surely that must be confirmation of what you have written. But I beg leave to continue my disagreement. And I hope I can make some progress in getting at what I think is the core of that disagreement.

First, about *facts*. You charge me with being in their grip. Well, I'm willing to consider objections to the term—and perhaps to the concept as well. As you and MacIntyre point out, our ancestors got along pretty well without the word for centuries. (Of course, that's true for many useful words, e.g., *culture*, which, outside of its agricultural meaning, dates from the nineteenth century.) But I think we can waive that discussion, or at least postpone it, for I plead not guilty to the charge, and to the related charge of being an unwitting Baconian, of being someone who thinks that "we could simply gaze at the facts of nature and the truth would emerge." For many years now I have found much to recommend itself in Thomas Kuhn's critique of that sort of simplistic scientific absolutism. And just a few years ago I published an article pointing out the interesting similarities between Kuhn's critique of science and that contained in C. S. Lewis's book, *The Discarded Image*. I wrote then:

> Lewis compares the investigation of nature to a forensic
> cross-examination in which a skilled attorney, without

"elicit[ing] falsehoods from an honest witness," will nevertheless determine "how much of [the] total truth will appear and what pattern it will suggest." In other words, given the vast multiplicity of natural objects, events and processes, it is impossible for a scientist to investigate each and every one of them in every possible way or to explore every lead theoretically open to him. The scientist works within the confines of a model which simultaneously guides and restricts his research choices. In short, we can say that "nature gives most of her evidence in answer to the questions we ask her."

But however much the critiques of both Lewis and Kuhn as applied to the scientific enterprise are correct, does this apply to our ordinary affairs, and if so, how? You say that "what we see in the world is dependent on what we choose to see." I can agree to some extent, in the sense that we often ignore things for one reason or another; indeed, we have to ignore many of the things around us, since of the multiplicity of events occurring around us, we cannot usually attend to all of them. But surely long before Bacon wrote, people spoke to each other unselfconsciously about what was happening around them, simply assuming they were experiencing more or less the same reality, the same external world. But let me focus my remarks by turning my attention to your discussion of history—and also of miracles, since I think they come under the same criteria of judgment.

I assume that you would agree that things happened in such and such a way. That is, there are no alternate realities. Things simply are, or (as in the case of history) simply were, simply occurred. However much we may make choices about which things we will attend to, there is only one reality. We say that someone suffering from mental illness is disconnected from reality, which presupposes that there *is* a reality and we'd best recognize that! If this is correct, then any difficulties in our ability to apprehend what did occur historically have to do with the limitations of human knowing, not with past events themselves. The post-Resurrection events recounted in the Gospels, for example, happened in one and only one way, even if we cannot completely disentangle the varying ways that the Evangelists narrate them. And of course historians have always known the difficulties that the historical record presents. Historical accounts are never complete, witnesses lie or forget, documents get lost or altered or even forged, we cannot look into the minds of historical actors to discover their motives, we have to rely upon what they said or did. But, as I said, historians have always known all this, and have tried to take these factors into account. Thus when you write, "No historian would give credence to an event seen only by those who have an interest in that event," I must dissent. Historians do it all the time. Of course, they attempt to adjust for the fact that the witnesses may be less than truthful, but very often the only accounts we have of events are those left by interested parties. So we look at possible motives for lying, we look at whatever light their actions, prior or subsequent, may throw on the event in question or on their characters, and so on. But we don't just reject it. Likewise, only an historian with a (probably hidden) bias against the supernatural will necessarily "conclude that [the disciples] hid the body." Certainly that is one hypothesis that must be examined, but it is his ideology that makes a historian reject the supernatural out of hand, not his credentials as an impartial historical researcher. And, to anticipate a possible objection on your part, a Christian historian might be led by an equally unconscious bias to examine the Gospel accounts more uncritically than he ought. Bias is possible for all of us, and we must be on our guard against it. But serious historians do regard the New Testament accounts as basically trustworthy, and moreover non-believers do come to accept the Gospels as truthful, conversions do occur, and sometimes these are based, in part at least, upon a consideration of the historical record, both in the New Testament and outside it.

What of miracles? For a Christian the questions of miracles cannot be divorced from history. In one of my prior letters I appealed to St. Paul's recounting of witnesses to the Resurrection in 1 Corinthians 15. Surely *he* was interested in the historicity of Christ's rising again. Indeed, he made it the touchstone of our faith: "if Christ has not been raised, then our preaching is in vain and your faith is in vain" (1 Corinthians 15:14). The whole tenor of his preaching and of his letters shows that he was not "offering a better story," but making an historical claim. You might reply that he proffered a story, and, yes, one can use that term. But story doesn't have a univocal meaning—and there can be stories that are not true, as you yourself note. Whether we want to call it a story or not, Paul was making historical claims, and he thought he could back them up with what we call historical evidence. The fact that Mormons likewise claim historical evidence does not mean that we should throw up our hands and start talking about how appealing our story is, versus theirs. No, it means it's time to roll up our sleeves and examine each account critically.

More about miracles though. It's not the case that "miracles are founded on the faith, and not the other way round." There are plenty of instances in the Gospels and in Acts of miracles having probative value. We might start with the Resurrection itself. The apostles were not believers when our

Lord appeared to them in the Cenacle. "But they were startled and frightened, and supposed that they saw a spirit" (Luke 24:37). Nor at Lystra when St. Paul healed a crippled man, and the local pagans, so far from having faith, or even obtaining faith, thought they recognized in Paul and Barnabas the gods Zeus and Hermes (Acts 14:8–13). Nor in many other examples which I could cite.

But let me turn my attention to what seems to be your criterion for judging among stories, namely, "which is more comprehensive and hence has greater explanatory power," as you say at one point, or "there are only good and bad stories, better and worse stories." This sort of criterion appears to me dangerously and hopelessly subjective. What one person finds good or interesting, another finds bad or boring. The story of God's creation, our Fall, God's redeeming acts and final return—the "Christian story"—appeals to some, but others find other stories more appealing, more interesting. Even the question of wider comprehensiveness is not clear. Could someone not claim that a syncretistic understanding of religion is more comprehensive than a merely Christian one? Why should we restrict our view of God's actions to one story only? Why not embrace them all in a larger and more comprehensive story? Unless—unless, our own story is historically true, we have no business condemning or rejecting other people's stories. It is difficult certainly to show someone that the New Testament narratives are historically sound, but I think it would be much more difficult to convince someone that they are in some sense better or more comprehensive or more appealing than the many other stories about. At least historicity is a touchstone, even if one that is sometimes elusive, whereas the other criteria seem to be purely subjective.

You say, "We cannot out-argue our modern pagans, we can only out-narrate them. We can only tell a better story, and we can only tell this story by living it. We don't convert the world because we don't live the story . . . love alone preaches the God who is love." Well, yes and no. Certainly if all Catholics lived their faith, things would be quite different, both inside and outside the Church. But look at one who did live that love. "I have shown you many good works from the Father; for which of these do you stone me?" (John 10:31). And ultimately they offered him the Cross. The world does not always respond favorably even to love, even to Love Himself.

In fact, the original conversion of the Roman world was accomplished by many means, including, though we don't like to dwell on it now, the new social atmosphere brought about by the official acceptance of the Faith by the imperial government. And in the conversion of northern Europe, it was usually the conversion of the king, after which his subjects naturally accepted the new doctrine, since the idea of individual religious opinion and choice, such as we take for granted in the modern world, was utterly unknown and unthinkable for people at that time. And in the case of a large portion of the Americas, it was the appearance of Our Lady of Guadalupe, a miracle with decided theological overtones for the Aztecs, not the conduct of their Spanish conquerors, loving or not.

What about today? People come into the Church for many reasons, some philosophical and historical, some biblical or theological, some liturgical, some on account of their attraction to the beauty and power of the Christian story, some on account of Christ's love shown in action. As Belloc wrote in his Foreword to G. K. Chesterton's *The Catholic Church and*

Conversion, "Men and women enter by every conceivable gate, after every conceivable process of slow intellectual examination, of shock, of vision, of moral trial and even of merely intellectual process." In other words, for a multiplicity of reasons. And this is fine. But we had better have an intellectually solid account at the ready for those who seek it. When, under stress, temptation, discouragement, whatever— when the attractiveness of our story wanes, we'd better be able to say to them, "But, hey, wait, it's true you know! It's more than a better story, it's a true one." If prelates fail to live up to it, if ordinary Catholics seem uninterested in it, that's not because it's no longer important. However well or ill we may live out our Faith, how much or how little our contemporaries may be fascinated by it, it is still true. We can never cease making that claim.

A very blessed and merry Christmas to you,

Thomas

REFERENCES

Hilaire Belloc, "Foreword," G. K. Chesterton, *The Catholic Church and Conversion*.

Thomas Storck, "Saving the Appearances? C. S. Lewis's Critique of Scientific Knowledge," *Sehnsucht* 10 (2016).

Letter 6

Knowledge and Faith: Which is Prior?

DEAR THOMAS,

I can't help but observe that you seem to want to have your cake and eat it too; you want to subject science to a critique of its claims, and then exempt the science of history from this critique. You ask if the critique applies to "things which simply occurred," and conclude that "there are no alternate realities." Well, I find that a doubtful proposition, even at the ontological level but certainly at the epistemological level. For the question is not so much what happened, but "how we can know what happened?" Or more importantly, why one event should be given more weight than another. And for these questions, there can never be a single "scientific" account. We can certainly say that whatever happened, happened, and that other things never happened at all. But how we can distinguish between the two and what that "happening" means will always reduce to judgments that escape the strict realm of science.

You want to root the validity of our Christian claims on the "historicity" of the Resurrection, but it is a question beyond history. You might as well set out to prove the Virgin Birth or the Immaculate Conception by purely historical means. But no such historical means exist, nor could exist;

71

the stories are accepted or rejected *sola fide*. And in the case of Christ, the problem is even greater: there are simply no contemporaneous accounts other than those of his followers. You say that historians accept such evidence all the time, but for the life of me I can't think of a single case. Indeed, historians don't deal in questions of miracles at all. You conclude that only an historian "with a (probably hidden) bias against the supernatural" could doubt these events. And while such a charge may stand against a purely secular or atheist historian, it cannot be sustained against, say, a Hindu or an Islamic historian. You might respond that they have a bias against Christianity. Fine, but then we are back to what I say, namely, that it is accepted as "history" only by believers; it is a "fact" of history only after being a judgment of faith.

Here's the problem you have: if you are going to accept the Resurrection as an historical reality independent of the beliefs of the observer and base this "reality" solely on the testimony of the Christian witnesses, then you are going to have to accept the historicity of the Book of Mormon or the appearance of Gabriel to Muhammad on the same grounds, or give us grounds to distinguish among these events. I do not think that is possible, but I invite you to give it a shot. And if you cannot give us grounds to distinguish these events—secure grounds why one should be accepted and the others rejected—then I don't see how the matter resolves to anything but faith: you believe Peter and Paul; you disbelieve Muhammad and Smith.

I do believe the Christian story to be more reasonable than all the others, but this is strictly a matter of judgment, of weighing evidence rather than of demonstrative proof. We must always be ready to give a reason for this faith of ours; we will never be able to give a demonstration. And frankly, I think the desire to engage in logical demonstrations can only work to undermine the real work of evangelization.

And there is a further difficulty. Even if there were unbelieving witnesses to the Resurrection, the historian still could not verify that it was not all just an elaborate hoax. There are reasons why Christ only appears to his disciples, to people who already have faith in him. And one of these reasons is that if he had shown himself to Pilate or to the Sanhedrin, they would likely only attempt to re-execute him as a fraud, a *doppelgänger* pretending to be the original. And that would not be an unreasonable conclusion; in like circumstances, you and I would be likely to do the same thing. In any case, what is beyond doubt is that there cannot be—by definition—a natural test for a supernatural event.

I cannot but think that you are appealing to the wrong issue, to the *facticity* of the Resurrection. But that is not in dispute, at least not between us; for both of us, this *facticity* is the foundation of our entire lives, including our religious and "scientific" lives. What is in dispute is whether this can be reached by any purely natural science, history included. The question remains, "Is knowledge of the Resurrection a matter of science or of faith?" Or put another way, "When people reject the Resurrection, are they being obtuse at best or anti-scientific at worst?" But if the Resurrection really was compelling in a scientific way, you would have to conclude that an awful lot of people are rejecting the clear evidence of their senses. Now, you can argue that way if you wish, but I'm pretty sure that you will convince only the already convinced and subject us all to ridicule if you can't distinguish the three cases I have mentioned.

You are still bothered by the term "story" because you find the judgment of them as good or bad to be too subjective.

For my part, that is not an objection at all; after all, it is the subjects we meet that we are trying to reach, starting with the subject I meet in the mirror. And all human knowledge is personal knowledge, subjective. We work to make it better but we are mistaken to think we can make it perfect. The hunger for "objectivity" will always leave one starving.

But even to the degree that your objection to stories is valid, it turns out to be less of a problem than you seem to think. For it always turns out that some stories are more enduring than others. Some stories rapidly gain a large audience, and are just as quickly forgotten; others endure through centuries. There were many poets in Homer's day, I should imagine, but only one which the generations sought to preserve. There have been many playwrights since Shakespeare, but Will has managed to speak to every generation since. Literature, it turns out, is far more stable in its judgments than is science. Science is always contingent; literature is enduring. The judgment of science is always "pending further developments." So even if you "proved" it today, it only means you might have to revise it tomorrow.

You dispute the idea that the stories that are called histories can be judged on the basis of which story is more comprehensive. I'm not quite sure I understand your objection, since the proposition seems self-evident. Surely, a history which can narrate the Civil War in terms both of Union and of slavery is likely to be more reliable than one that reduces it to either Union or slavery. I don't see how that can be doubted. But it seems to be that your doubts arise from a fear of syncretism. However, I find that syncretism is less of a problem since such stories rarely hold anyone's attention for very long. Syncretism is a game for intellectuals who think that they can rationalize the contending claims. It simply doesn't work, precisely because it doesn't produce a coherent or interesting story. However, contending stories do get synthesized, and the Church is more than willing to do this in matters that touch practices but not the core; we are quite happy to accept Easter eggs and Christmas trees, or to replace the pantheon of gods, each with his or her own special domain, with a canon of saints, each with his or her own special patronage. And Christian philosophy is built on the pagan *logoi spermatikoi*, the "seeds of the word" which remain at the root of much Christian theorizing. And it also worked in the opposite direction, since at least some pagans—Plotinus, for example—were more than willing to borrow from the Christians. All religion beyond the most primitive is synthetic, including Christianity, which is why we have an Old Testament.

And the Old Testament itself is "synthetic," the development of a millennium at least. For example, there is no mention of the resurrection of the dead until the Judeans come in contact with the Persian Empire and its Zoroastrianism, where resurrection and a final battle between good and evil are foundational. This lack of any mention of the resurrection of the dead puts Jesus in a rather tight situation when the Sadducees question him about the resurrection (Mark 12:18–27). But rather than cite the rather obvious examples, such as Ezekiel and the field of dry bones (Ezek 37:1–14), Jesus can answer them only from the Pentateuch, because that is the only literature they accept. But there is nothing in those books to support his case, so he gives a rather tendentious reading of Exodus 3:6. The point is this: without the "syncretism" of the Judean and Persian religions, there would be no basis in the Old Testament for the central doctrine of the New. In the same way, without pagan philosophy, Christian theology would be truly impoverished, so impoverished that this conversation would be unimaginable.

In any case, let me state my case: for human beings, faith is prior to knowledge. The materialist, no less than the theist, ultimately rests his knowledge in a faith that is beyond proof. He asserts that all can be explained by the motions of matter (which still leaves matter unexplained); the Christian responds that all things can be explained by the will of God (which still leaves God unexplained). And if Gödel's incompleteness theorem and Tarski's undefinability theorem are correct, this problem extends even to the realms of mathematics and logic. Even the logician requires a naïve faith; even the mathematician can doubt that his numbers really add up.

But I do not think we will resolve this question, at least not directly. So what to do? How to continue? Let me suggest that instead of trying to resolve the difference, we embrace it. We take it as two poles of a further discussion, two approaches to some fundamental questions of Christianity, society, politics, or what you will. The starting positions are far enough apart to provide what should be an interesting conversation, or at least interesting to me and perhaps to you, even if to no one else.

So what should we call these contrasting positions? Yours could be called, with no little justice, the *rationalist* position. That term, however, so reasonable in itself, has acquired some baggage which is not so reasonable, and it would not be reasonable to lay it upon you. So let me suggest we use the term *scholastic*, a term which I judge has a better ring to your ears, even if to me there is really little substantive difference between the two terms.

As for my position, one could with justice call it the *fideist* position, but that term too has some unpleasant baggage, so I would prefer, if it's all the same to you, that we call it the *mystical* position. And starting from these two fundamental and contrasting approaches, the scholastic and the mystical, we approach some fundamental questions. Perhaps we could start at one end, and see how we view this very odd fellow, Jesus the Nazorean, odd in that he is one person with two natures. So is he the divine rationalist knowing "scientifically" all things past and present, which imparts a knowledge that enlightens his human nature? Or is he a human mystic who through faith accesses his divine nature to enlighten the faith of humanity? Or we could start at the opposite end, with modernity and how it is overcome, or not, by the contending starting points of view. Or we could start somewhere in the middle.

I leave the choice to you. This reverses the procedure; instead of you responding to my original essay, you fire the opening shot and I will take cover and return fire as best I can.

How does that sound?

John

Letter 7

Dear John,

I think your suggestion about making a new start in this dialogue is a good one. I have, it is true, some reluctance about not replying to your latest in detail. But perhaps in our further conversation much of what I would have said will come out anyway. I will, though, make one point and one only, as much by way of clarification as of argument: I did not claim that anything like a *demonstration* (in the scholastic sense) of the Resurrection, or indeed of any historical event, can be made. The proper places for demonstrations are philosophical or theological discussions. History is different, though this does not mean that it need be subjective or a matter of faith. But its methods and standards are different from those of philosophy. But enough on this. Let me take up your challenge to start over with "modernity and how it is overcome, or not, by [our] contending starting points of view." So let's start with that, with modernity and all that that implies, which is certainly quite a handful.

Modernity is a subject I've written about more than once, so I feel some confidence in talking about it. But what is it and how to describe it? It certainly can be characterized in different ways, but for my purposes here I'll call attention to one of the most pervasive features of modernity, the widespread decline of religious faith and practice. I don't think there can be much debate that such a decline has occurred— on a massive scale, and one that began not a few decades ago, but rather centuries, and in a more complex manner than many people think. For beginning about the sixteenth century the Church lost control of one social or cultural sector after another: the political, the economic, the artistic, and finally in our time, the familial and personal.

But there was a sort of break in this gloomy series of events. Starting late in the eighteenth century and lasting until just after the middle of the twentieth, the Church did seem to be regaining some of her cultural standing. The tide did seem to be turning to some extent. What had happened? Although originally this Catholic revival seemed grounded merely in the Romantic movement, with its interest in the Middle Ages, in folk cultures, in all that the rationalist eighteenth century despised or neglected, this changed after the election of Leo XIII as pope in 1878. Leo furnished a stronger foundation for this still nascent Catholic revival, and provided a kind of official "strategy" for it, a strategy of how to meet the challenges of modernity. This strategy, embraced more or less by the entire Church, continued by Leo's successors for nearly a century, implemented with more or less intelligence, fervor, and success, was one of the most remarkable events in the life of the modern Church.

What was this strategy? On the one hand, it was a restatement of the essentials of the Faith, a setting aside of certain inessential elements that had accrued to it, all with an eye to the ways of thinking, problems, concerns, and issues of vital importance to modern man. In this there was no compromise on essentials, no suggestion that the ancient Faith needed watering down, but a frank willingness to dispense with certain contingent points that had too often been regarded as constituent parts of a Catholic apologetic, e.g., reflexive support for monarchical government or insistence on papal sovereignty over central Italy.

Vital to this effort was Leo's deliberate call to place the philosophical and theological foundations of the revival in the philosophy of St. Thomas, or *scholasticism* as you say. For Leo well understood that it is philosophy "upon which the foundation of other sciences in great measure depends," as he wrote in his first encyclical letter, a subject to which, the very next year, he devoted an entire encyclical. Although one might think that after several centuries in which thinkers such as Descartes, Hume, and Kant had had free rein, the thought of St. Thomas would be hopelessly inadequate and outdated, this proved not to be the case. By being willing to argue from first principles, Thomists could and did confront the philosophies of the past several centuries.

And this policy or strategy was successful. Not totally, certainly, but in the period of the implementation of this program, the Faith, which had been battered for centuries, did seem to be growing stronger, to be regaining, to some degree, its former cultural standing. There were numerous conversions of important intellectuals. Catholic thought was no longer ignored, but usually given a respectful attention. Becoming a Catholic was now widely viewed as a perfectly legitimate, if still a bit daring, option.

There is no need here to describe how we ourselves destroyed this revival, nor to point out how what we've done since has clearly not been especially successful. But my point is that something like Leo's program is the kind of action we need to take if we are to have any hope of overcoming modernity. It seems rather unlikely now, I must admit, that we could undertake anything like this again, sort of like putting toothpaste back into the tube. But this is how I read things. A vital engagement with the world, with its thought, but from a secure and above all, confident, Catholicism, with a sound philosophical basis in Thomas, is what we need. If it could happen, it might achieve more than we can imagine.

Thomas

REFERENCE

Leo XIII, Encyclical *Inscrutabili Dei Consilio*, n. 13.

Letter 8

"The Clarity of
a Despotic Logic"

Dear Thomas,

Your letter illustrates one of the main points we have been discussing so far, namely how different persons can examine the same history and come to widely differing conclusions. You look at the history of modernity and find a call for a revival of scholasticism; I look at scholasticism and find the root of modernism. For if we are to confront modernity, we must first confront its history and define what it is. And when we do that we find that modern liberalism is the highest achievement of the Middle Ages, even if that achievement has managed to negate itself. Only by understanding what it is, where it came from, and how it negated itself can we hope to rescue it from its own excesses.

It is true that there was a revival of interest in the. Middle Ages after the disasters of the French Revolution, and largely as a reaction against it, but this revival had little to do with scholasticism. After Catholicism had lost its political significance, it was "safe" to examine it without getting mired in political disputes. Its revival was not so much philosophical as it was aesthetic and liturgical. Thomism became ascendant only by papal decree, which is never a good foundation for a movement unless the decree is already embodied in the wider Church culture. I'm not convinced it was, or should be. Why one would want to reduce the richness of Christian theology to one particular method (dialectics) and one particular period is beyond me.

And further, it fails to recognize Thomas himself as the radical he was, the "post-modernist" of his own day, arousing the suspicions of the more "traditionalist" elements of the Church. This attitude is attested by Étienne Tempier and the Condemnation of 1277. Our current battles are very reminiscent of this one, with the "traditionalists" confronting the "modernists," and doing so with doubtful accusations and wildly exaggerated claims. Of the 404 propositions condemned by Tempier, the Bishop of Paris and former chancellor of the Sorbonne, few were actually held by the scholastics and perhaps none in the form in which Tempier stated them. But Tempier was not entirely wrong; there was a danger in the Aristotelian rationalism of the scholastics. Thomas, reading Aristotle through the lenses of Ibn Rushd and Ibn Sina (and it is important to give their real, rather than Latinized, names) introduced a totalizing logic with the fond hope that competing positions could be synthesized through the use of a dialectic methodology. It is not quite correct to say that Thomas argued from "first principles"; rather, his arguments begin in Sacred Scripture, or at least he claims that they do. It is solely for this reason that his *summa* of philosophy could rightly be titled a *Summa theologiae*. But it was very much a scripture subjected to the norms of "reason," one that would relegate the irrational to the margins. But this only allowed the irrational to assume new and more pernicious forms; when you attempt to rationalize everything, you discover that anything can be rationalized. Thus, it is not surprising at all that the notorious *Malleus maleficarum* ("The Hammer of Witches") was written in the form of a *summa*. But Christianity is not about the rational; the Passion is not rational, nor are the Eucharist, the Incarnation, the Virgin Birth, or the Resurrection. All must be seen as transcending any human logic.

So how should we approach the task of confronting modernity? I think we should start by recognizing that modernity is the supreme accomplishment of the Middle Ages and then ask, "What went wrong?" When we think of modernity, we think of individualism, natural rights, democracy, and rationalism, particularly in the form of scientism.

Perhaps no idea is more associated with Liberalism than the idea of *individualism*, the idea of the transcendent dignity of the person, possessing his or her own will and a value independent of social position. This idea is central to the Christian message. It is easy to forget today just how profoundly Christianity altered the relationship between the individual and the world. For antiquity, the world was eternal but individuals were transient. The *polis* or *civitas* was regarded as potentially eternal (e.g., "Eternal Rome") and collapsed only because of sin and decadence in its members. Thus Aristotle could place the state over the citizen and even the virtues had a mainly civic function of ensuring peace. The transitory individual was a threat to the endurance of the state, ethics were enclosed by politics, and the individual was a mere passing instance of a more general (and enduring) type.

The Christian message changed all of that: empires come and go, but each person has an incomparable dignity and an everlasting destiny. The cramped civic virtues of moderation were supplemented by the theological virtue of charity, which is an overflowing, always an "excess." Moreover, each person, bearing a name, was in a sense a "species unto himself," unique and unrepeatable. The world itself is a mere passing shadow, the person an eternal reality. The human person, now liberated from the accidents of birth that bound him or her to a social status, could make a free decision to join the new Christian community. "Who is my mother? Who are my brothers? . . . Whoever does the will of my heavenly Father is my brother, and sister, and mother" (Matt 12:48–50). That is to say, by a free act of the will, the *individual* could escape the bounds of conformity to a social status and join a community not based on class or blood. The idea of natural rights, as in Thomas Paine's *The Rights of Man*, has become associated with modernity, but in fact, it emerged in the Middle Ages and in the development of canon law, a law that transcended the ethnic and class-based laws of particular nations and applied to king and commoner, prince and peasant alike. As Brian Tierney put it: "Medieval people first struggled for survival; then they struggled for rights." By 1300 a number of particular rights were regularly defended in terms of natural law. They would include rights to property, rights of consent to government, rights of self-defense, rights of infidels, marriage rights, and procedural rights.

Democracy has its roots in monasticism, self-governing communities where individuals freely submit to the rule of an abbot they themselves have elected. Moreover, the monasteries represented the ideals of moral equality replacing "natural" inequality, and the dignity of labor replacing the notion that physical labor was "servile." The ideals of self-government spread from monastic rule to corporate law (as in guilds or cities). Here, the corporation was no longer necessarily a creature of public authority, but could be founded by any group apart from the state. And authority flowed upward from the members to the officers, and even then, the officers had to get the consent of the members for certain decisions.

From the corporation and the monasteries, the idea of self-government would spread to the cities, which achieved their independence from the feudal lords and became self-governing corporations, with ultimate authority lodged in an assembly of people. The cities established a new class of persons, one that stood between the serf and the nobles: the middle or bourgeoisie. The cities became the locus of freedom, where a runaway serf who could evade capture for a year and a day became a freeman: "the air of the city makes free."

This brief analysis could be extended to many areas, but it should be sufficient to show that Liberalism is not, in itself, something alien to the Christian experience, but rather something that arises from it. Indeed, by the fourteenth and early fifteenth centuries, Liberalism had been firmly established, rooted in four fundamental principles: natural equality was the only basis for a legal system; moral conduct had to be a free act of the will; the individual had natural rights and hence a degree of liberty; and only a representative government was appropriate for free men.

There is one historical thread that flows through all of these principles: as they moved further from their Christian roots, they became more and more secularized, that is, divorced from their roots. And like any plant separated from its roots, it became perverse. Under the influence of the purely secular notions of the Enlightenment, the ancient Christian ideals of *liberté, égalité, fraternité* became weaponized and turned against their founders, leading to the Terror and the Vendée. The people who longed for liberty, equality, and fraternity ended up getting, as Marx noted, "cavalry, infantry, and artillery."

But what is it that opened up the space for secularism? That is the great question. And only when we answer that question can we search for ways to close the space and reunite the modern order with its medieval roots. My contention is that this space is opened up precisely by Thomistic rationalism and specifically by Thomas's divorce of faith and reason. Thomas asserts that a thing "cannot be seen and believed at the same time" (ST 2-2.1.4 ad 2), "hence it is equally impossible for one and the same thing to be an object of science and of belief" (ST 2-2.1.5). Further, although faith is a virtue, it is paradoxically one shared by the demons (ST 2-2.5.2), but not by the angels (ST 2-2.5.1), nor is it shared with the blessed in heaven, since perfect understanding is not compatible with faith (ST 2-2.8.2). That is, faith and science are mutually exclusive such that more of one means less of the other. And finally, at the beatific vision, our faith will be completely displaced by science. Thus for Thomas faith is a stopgap, and the gap is clearly our sinful and ignorant condition. Faith fills that gap, but only until something better comes along, namely knowledge; as the gaps are closed, the domain of faith diminishes, and here we see the genesis of the "God of the gaps." At the end of time faith disappears entirely and we have a vision of the divine essence (ST 1-2.3.8) and obtain perfect knowledge of it (ST 1-2.4.3), a knowledge without the gaps and hence without the faith. But while we walk the earth, we need faith, a need that will diminish in time and eventually disappear. Faith may have a certain priority in the world, but actual priority belongs properly to science. Whatever the temporal exigencies may be, there is a clear priority in Thomas of *knowing* over *believing*; faith is ultimately subordinate to science. Indeed, the order found in St. Paul is reversed; it is not knowledge that will pass away (1 Cor 13:8) while faith abides (1 Cor 13:13), but precisely the opposite: knowledge will be all and faith nothing.

Regardless of what one thinks of this approach, it cannot be denied that it opens up a purely secular space. For it is but a small step to push for an expansion of knowledge—and hence a diminution of faith—in this world, and not relegate the whole process to the next. This allows for a purely *secular* knowledge which will dispense with the need for faith. It is on this hope that all of modern scientism rests. Everything that comes after rests on this view, and this view can point in only one direction, the direction we have travelled. Hence I do not see how Thomism can be both cause and cure; it is like a drunk trying to sober up with another shot of gin.

All that being said, there is a school of thought that is trying to follow your advice and cure modernism with a Thomistic physic. This is the Radical Orthodoxy school led by John Milbank, which attempts to use the post-modernist critique of modernism to destroy the modernist hegemony, while giving Thomas a post-modernist interpretation. I remain skeptical that such a reading of Thomas will be recognizable to Thomists, but then I know quite a few Thomists, all of whom are more knowledgeable of the Angelic Doctor than I am, who subscribe to this approach. But of this I am convinced: it cannot be a reading of scholasticism that purports to provide "the clarity of a despotic logic" (as Philipp Rosemann terms it) in place of faith. For in such a pure logic, only secularism can flourish.

Best regards,
John

REFERENCES

Hannah Arendt, *The Life of the Mind: Willing*, one-volume edition (New York: Harvest/HBJ, 1978), 66.

Aristotle, *Politics*, VII, 17, 1336 a25–30.

Theology: Mythos or Logos?

John Milbank, *Theology and Social Theory: Beyond Secular Reason* (Oxford: Blackwell Publishers, 1990), 360.

Larry Siedentop, *Inventing the Individual: The Origins of Western Liberalism* (Cambridge: Belknap Press of Harvard University, 2017), 234, 247, 269–74, 331.

Brian Tierney, *The Idea of Natural Rights* (Grand Rapids: Eerdmans, 1977), 55.

Letter 9

Dear John,

As usual you raise numerous interesting points, and as usual, I have to demur. First, a couple of items for the sake of clarity. I quoted Leo XIII in my previous letter to the effect that it is philosophy "upon which the foundation of other sciences in great measure depends," words from his first encyclical, *Inscrutabili*, of 1878. And I noted that Thomists sought "to argue from first principles" in their engagement with modern thought. Thus it was *philosophy* that I was talking about, not theology, so when you say, "It is not quite correct to say that Thomas argued from 'first principles'; rather, his arguments begin in Sacred Scripture, or at least he claims that they do," I think you were missing my point. It's certainly the case that Thomas was a professional theologian, and his purely philosophical works were more or less incidental to his theological career, but they are, nevertheless, works of philosophy, not of theology, and it was as such that Pope Leo thought they could be of use to the Church's apostolate in the last quarter of the nineteenth century, and which, in my estimation, they continued to be well afterwards. For, however one understands or explains it, there *was* a Catholic revival, and what I claimed for it is a matter of historical record. Though it did begin as part of the Romantic reaction against the eighteenth century, the philosophical foundation that Leo XIII gave it in Thomism was not simply an instance of papal fiat, for interest in Aquinas had been percolating, especially in Italy and Germany, decades before Leo came to the papacy in 1878. And whatever awkward or incongruent aspects there were to this renewed Thomism at the outset, they were continually being corrected or refined as Catholic philosophers came to understand Thomas better and to adopt his modes of thought and terminology more closely.

But this brings up some other points. "Why," you say, "one would want to reduce the richness of Christian theology to one particular method (dialectics) and one particular period is beyond me." But is there not some confusion here? First, if by the dialectic method you mean the mode of arguing used, say, in the *Summa theologiae*—a work of *theology*, moreover—this was not used by Aquinas always, and seldom in his purely philosophical writing, nor generally by many of the Thomists of later centuries. And again, it was philosophy that I was talking about here. The fact that that philosophy began in "one particular period" would not seem to have any bearing on its truth or falsity. If Thomas's fundamental philosophical approach is correct, then it is that which matters, not when or where he wrote. Moreover Thomas was part of a much longer and vibrant tradition of thought that traces itself all the way back to Thales and the other Pre-Socratics via Plato to Aristotle and his commentators, and which many other Thomists continued to develop long after the death of the Angelic Doctor.

But perhaps more important is another thing you say, namely that my wish for another Thomistic revival "fails to recognize Thomas himself as the radical he was, the 'postmodernist' of his own day, arousing the suspicions of the more 'traditionalist' elements of the Church." Nothing here I would necessarily deny. Thomas was indeed a "radical," but a radical in the sense that he sought to discover the roots of the questions he investigated, something which is especially clear in his philosophical teachings. His use of the newly-translated expanded corpus of Aristotle's writings came not from a desire for novelty, but from a desire for truth. His activity did indeed arouse the suspicions of conservative elements in the Church, a point, by the way, which shows how *conservatism* as such can never be an adequate criterion of our thinking or for discovering truth. Because Thomas looked to Aristotle, whose works, beyond a portion of the *Organon*, were then first becoming known to western Europe, some have argued that the Church should always embrace the philosophical currents of the day. But this misses the point. Thomas used Aristotle not because Aristotle was a novelty, but because he thought that in Aristotle's philosophy could be found the fundamentally correct approach to understanding reality.

Now, finally, I come to your main point, that "modernity is the supreme accomplishment of the Middle Ages." You say this based on your claim that certain of the practices or institutions associated with modernity were present in the Middle Ages: "natural equality was the only basis for a legal system; moral conduct had to be a free act of the will; the individual had natural rights and hence a degree of liberty; and only a representative government was appropriate for free men."

I will not quibble about the presence of such ideas or practices in the Middle Ages, at least not about the first three items in your list. But what I will quibble about, nay, strongly disagree about, is the leap you make from the presence of such things to the presence of *Liberalism*. "Indeed, by the fourteenth and early fifteenth centuries, Liberalism had been firmly established, rooted in four fundamental principles," namely, the four I just quoted from you. It is not the mere presence of such principles that is decisive, but what they *meant*, what part they played in the complex of ideas, attitudes, practices, and institutions that comprise a culture. Indeed, some of these ideas and practices are hardly unique to either the Middle Ages or to modernity.

> Our constitution . . . favours the many instead of the few; this is why it is called a democracy. If we look to the laws, they afford equal justice to all in their private differences; advancement in public life falls to reputation for capacity, class considerations not being allowed to interfere with merit; nor again does poverty bar the way, if a man is able to serve the state, he is not hindered by the obscurity of his condition. The freedom which we enjoy in our government extends also to our ordinary life. There, far from exercising a jealous surveillance over each other, we do not feel called upon to be angry with our neighbour for doing what he likes, or even to indulge in those injurious looks which cannot fail to be offensive, although they inflict no positive penalty.

These words, of course, are from Pericles's famous Funeral Oration of 430 BC, as found in Thucydides. Here also you have some of the traits that you associate particularly with Liberalism or modernity, but at a time and place far removed from the modern spirit. Do I claim that we can find here intact the modern spirit? By no means. But I do claim that forms and institutions, such as democratic voting, equal rights, etc. can exist and have existed in other contexts, not as precursors of modernity.

Of course, since modernity did follow the Middle Ages chronologically, after somewhat of a transitional period, there had to be something in the Middle Ages that led to modernity. Otherwise we'd have to say that it just jumped up suddenly out of nowhere. So, yes, by the end of the Middle Ages certain traits characteristic of modernity can be discerned—but are they its "supreme accomplishment" or its supreme betrayal? It was nominalism, in my view, that played that role, but only by denying the real supreme achievements of the Middle Ages.

Nominalism at first had little influence on political and social institutions, but in time the intellectual corrosion that it contained did lead, sometimes by a tortuous route, to modernity or Liberalism. In the political realm it gave birth to the idea of the state of nature and the social contract, placing human good outside of society and especially outside of the state. Political society becomes then a mere contrivance to guarantee the individual liberty which we bring with us from the so-called state of nature, and as a result social authority has no business with anything except what will preserve or enhance those individual liberties. As another result, and one of the greatest importance, within society the various spheres of human life, political, economic, educational, even religious, each went its own way, pursuing what it considered its own proper end, but not as part of a hierarchy of ends and means that reached its apex in God, as was characteristic of the medieval thinking. *This* is what marks modernity or Liberalism, and the gradual reduction of religious influence from the social order is nothing but a working out of the original seed, planted by the nominalists and watered by political philosophers from Hobbes to Rousseau.

It was not Thomas nor his distinction—hardly a divorce—between faith and reason, that opened the way to modernity. Indeed, such a distinction is implicit in Sacred Scripture itself. For if we can know that God *is* by means of his creation, as St. Paul taught in Romans 1:19–20, and if in addition "God spoke of old to our fathers by the prophets; but in these last days he has spoken to us by a Son" (Hebrews 1:1–2), then what is this except the distinction between those things that are accessible to reason and those things that have been revealed and hence, strictly speaking, are matters of faith? None of this brings about modernity or a "secular space," unless you consider as secular whatever is not a matter of revealed truth. But there is a natural world which is open to our senses and to our reason. To recognize that is not to be a secularist. It all depends upon how we regard that world, what we want to do in and with it. Modernity, following its initial impetus, has chosen to manipulate and twist that natural reality according to its ever-present desire to dominate in the interests of what is indeed a despotism, but a despotism not of logic but of pure individual will. "The End of our Foundation is the knowledge of Causes, and secret motions of things and the enlarging of the bounds of Human Empire, to the effecting of all things possible," as one of the Fathers of Salomon's House, a sort of research institute, in Francis Bacon's fable *New Atlantis* puts it. Here modernity works itself out, and there is a clear trajectory from the state of nature doctrine of Hobbes and Locke and Rousseau, through the alleged right of each one to the pursuit of happiness, to the mutilation of the human body celebrated today in the name of freedom, but in reality in subservience to one's disordered will. The freedom to create one's own reality, so far from being anything in the thought of St. Thomas, is the end result of nominalism's focus on the individual and its rejection of the reality of anything of a higher order.

Enough for now, and I look forward to your reply.

My best, as always,

Thomas

REFERENCES

Francis Bacon, *New Atlantis.*
Thucydides, *History of the Peloponnesian War*, Book II, 37.

Letter 10

Unless You Believe,
You Will Not Understand

Dear Thomas,

I certainly agree with Leo XIII that Thomas is the foundation for modern science; I think there is a direct line between Thomas Aquinas and Isaac Newton, with stops along the way at Buridan, Descartes, and Bacon. In fact, I think that's the whole problem with modern science, since faith (meaning) and reason have become separated, which is bad, and reason elevated over faith, which is disastrous.

As for philosophy, claims to begin with "first principles" or to be "aiming at the truth" are banal, if not outright pretentious; everybody claims that. Do you know of any philosopher who claims to start with secondary principles or to be aiming at error? In any case, "first principles" and demonstrative reason apply only to the formal realms of mathematics and (perhaps) metaphysics; for the material world we work with practical reason, and "first principles" become a suspicious category. We must derive higher principles from our experience of the world, and this experience will always be conditioned on what we have been conditioned to see. Furthermore, the conclusions of practical reason are always provisional, always pending further information. More on this anon.

I am a bit puzzled by your claim that Thomas used dialectics only in theology. It is certainly the method of the *Summas*, which are mostly philosophical, despite the title. Thomas was a prolific writer and I have not read all his works, so perhaps you can enlighten me on works that rely on another method. But be that as it may, dialectics cannot be the primary method of theology. Theology is always a literary and contemplative endeavor. In some cases, especially in philosophy, dialectics are helpful, but in theology they are not primary. For this reason, I think Thomas was a better philosopher than he was a theologian. At least some of his theology is problematic, such as his strict predestinationism (indistinguishable from what Calvinism would become), or his asserting two wills in God (which Luther would later assert), or his demotion of faith to a mere stopgap (which is the primary assumption of scientism). Indeed, one can derive the whole dismal "TULIP" of Calvinism without ever leaving the bounds of the *Summa*. This is not to demonize Thomas, but it is to protest the deification of Thomism, the reduction of the long history of Christian philosophy to one philosopher. Like any other, he had his insights and moments of brilliance, as well as his failures and contradictions. In truth, there is no "Catholic" philosophy, there is only philosophy enlightened by Christianity, an enlightenment that will take many forms and follow many paths.

To your point about political theory, it is of course true that all of the themes, save one, taken up by medieval politics had antecedents in the ancient world, indeed in every world, since these are basic to humanity itself. But Christianity added something that would be impossible in the ancient world, something that was startling and revolutionary: a strong notion of individual dignity and the human will. The classical world found no will in the person, most likely because they knew nothing at all about personhood. This world gave preeminence to types rather than to individuals. Only the species was stable and had permanence; the individual was merely an instantiation of a given nature, a "type." The city was regarded as "eternal" (i.e., "Eternal Rome") and fell only through the failure of individuals to perform to type. Individuals themselves are of value only in so far as they reflect the fullness of the type. Antiquity gave the name "virtue" to this fulfillment of destiny within any given existing thing. A "virtuous" tree was all that a tree should be. Ultimately, a virtuous man was all that a man should be.

It would remain thus until the advent of Christianity, because the event of Christ, as understood by Christians, raises questions that are simply not possible in the pagan world. If Christ was one person subsisting in two natures, then there must be a distinction between "person" and "nature." A person then emerges not as a mere instantiation of a nature, but as an individual with a nature at his service. Nature answers the question "What am I?" whereas person answers the question "Who am I?" As Frederick Wilhelmsen puts it:

> Only persons, strictly speaking, are named. Individuals sharing sub-human natures are simply units within the real, more or less perfect depending on their having fulfilled the potentialities of their natures. . . . To be a person suggests not only having a name—spies and criminals, after all, often have a half dozen names—but *being* a name.

Human freedom—and hence the human will—poses a problem for Greek antiquity because there is no notion of absolute beginning; there are no *new* series. Everything is but the working out of *potentialities* already contained in natures.

Even the world itself is eternal and the problem of an absolute beginning would not arise until the biblical doctrine of creation (although even this depends on adding *ex nihilo* to the biblical account). Time merely unfolds in act the potency already existing in natures. This resolution of everything that exists to potency and act works very well for certain things. The acorn has the potential of becoming an oak tree, and the oak the potential of producing acorns. There is no space in this description for freedom and certainly not for will; it would be a very willful oak indeed that produced olives instead of acorns.

But the human person is precisely that kind of "oak tree" that can will the olive rather than the acorn. He can surprise us, or rather we can surprise ourselves by doing something entirely unexpected and new, something not reducible to potentiality, a truly "new series." For example, he can write a symphony. And this symphony really is a "new thing," not reducible to some prior potency. As Hannah Arendt puts it:

> But the insufficiency of the Aristotelian explanation is evident: Can anyone seriously maintain that the symphony produced by a composer was "possible before it was actual"?—unless one means by "possible" no more than that it was clearly not impossible, which of course is entirely different from it having existed in a state of potentiality, waiting for some musician who would take the trouble to make it actual.

Christianity added this strong notion of the individual. C. S. Lewis perfectly captured the new Christian view of the person:

> There are no ordinary people. You have never talked to a mere mortal. Nations, cultures, arts, civilizations—

these are mortal, and their life is to ours as the life of a gnat. But it is immortals whom we joke with, work with, marry, snub and exploit. . . . Next to the Blessed Sacrament itself, your neighbor is the holiest object presented to your senses.

And it is in the Middle Ages that this strong notion of the individual reaches its height, a height expressed in law as "natural rights." After all, it is in the Christian West that iconography becomes portraiture and poetry becomes personal. This has tremendous political implications, and what it implies is precisely what we call "Liberalism." Of course, "Liberalism" is an ambiguous term, first used to describe an economic system, a system that itself would be the death of liberalism. And it is the death of liberalism because it claims to operate in a morally neutral space, while liberalism was and is, if anything, madly moral. Nevertheless, we can use the term for the bundle of rights that rise in the Middle Ages, and largely arise through canon law.

Law was a problem in the Middle Ages because it was tribal. It was said that you could have five people walking together down the street, and each would be covered by a different law because they belonged to different nations. This played havoc with the Church's ability to appoint its own clergy, control its own revenues, and manage its own affairs; it had to deal with innumerable codes and authorities that made administration a nightmare. The response was canon law, a universal law that transcended tribe and class and subjected all men and all nations to its rules, and did so on an equal basis. So successful was the Church at centralizing its governance and revenues that the secular rulers wanted the same thing for their realms, since they faced the same problems. They hired canon lawyers to write national codes of law, overriding the innumerable local and tribal codes, and were able, like the Vatican, to centralize revenues and administration in capital cities, whose main job was administration and tax collection. And it is on this basis of rights codified in a universal (or at least national) law that the modern polity is founded.

As for how that view became secularized, I think you give nominalism too much influence and too much weight. In fact, philosophy, whether Thomist or Ockhamist, is always a trailing indicator; societies change and then look around for ideas which make sense of the change. The early Middle Ages grew in its ability to bring the world under the reign of reason, and discovered Aristotle as the useful tool, forgetting why the Greeks had more or less abandoned him. But the world developed in less than rational ways, as it always does, and difference became the social problem. Thus Scotus could be more concerned with *haecceity* rather than *quiddity*, with "thisness" rather than "whatness." The world needed some sort of explanation of difference in a world where difference came to dominate. Or again, is capitalism greedy because of the ideas of Mandeville, or was Mandeville providing a rationale for what was already a social fact? I'm going with the latter.

The philosopher emphasized essences, but these are problematic in the world of time. What is the "essence" of the horse? Is it the eohippus or the Arabian? The Clydesdale or the Mongolian pony? And if I am a horse breeder, do I give a whit for the "essence" of the horse? No, I care only about the particularities of the mare and the stallion in relation to the qualities I wish to produce. My own position (for what that's worth) is neither essentialist nor particularistic, but historic: the essence of the horse is the history of the horse, a history that is not yet complete; it includes the eohippus and the pony, and everything in-between and everything yet to come; that is to say, its essence is not yet complete.

This has implications for the human person. Only God *is* being; man is more of a *becoming*. Only Yahweh can say, "I am who am"; man says, "I am that which I shall become." For we are always in the process of creating our own personhood, one that is unique to us and not a mere type or species. Man in his mind may be Parmenides; but in his life, he is Heraclitus, always in flux and change, and tending towards death. He transcends nature, but this transcendence is always pointing to the future and consummated only in the last moment, or beyond. And this is true of all beings in time; they possess not so much being as becoming.

Now, I take it that you (like the scientists) would like man to create this personality according to the dictates of reason, and that if he could just grasp the "first principles" and correctly apply the methods of reason, he would reach the correct identity. I find that unreasonable, or at least unlikely. And I am suspicious of any claims to have done so. I find that a man is never so biased as when he thinks himself "objective"; never so reliant on judgments as when he thinks he relies only on "facts." For the truth about human reasoning is that what a man considers "reasonable" is dependent on what stories he carries around about the workings of the world. Each of us carries this narrative. The materialist has a narrative that resolves all things to the motion of matter and the theist one that resolves all things to the Will of God. What falls within these stories will appear to each as "reasonable" and what falls outside as "superstition." That is to say, reason is not its own ground, at least not in the human person. We simply don't work that way. Each side in these debates believes itself to be reasonable because it is; but it is not a reason that is communicable to the other side. So, it is faith in the story that undergirds all reason, and not the other way round.

Thomas, I think, believed as you do. He treats reason as final and faith as a stopgap. You say this is a "distinction" and not a "divorce," but Thomas is emphatic on the matter: the same thing cannot be both seen and believed; it is one or the other but never both. But *sed contra*, I respond, it is both or it is neither. And it is first faith and only after reason, because reason depends on faith and cannot exist apart from it. It may not depend on our faith, and most commonly doesn't. But I refuse to let anyone get away with saying their *Zeitgeist* is independent of their faith; that's just not possible. Further, I find your interpretation of Hebrews 1:1 to be problematic at best. How does the appearance of the Son make things reducible to reason rather than faith, since you can only know that he is Son through faith, something the New Testament makes clear over and over again? Certainly, the Son never makes the claim that you make. Rather, the methods of the Son are precisely the methods of the prophets: prayer, parable, prophecy, psalm, sermon, and sign. He gives us a Sermon on the Mount, not a seminar in the synagogue; he gives us signs and wonders, not *Summa*s and tracts. And I assume he gives us the best gifts possible, the gift that is more basic. I stand with St. Augustine: unless you believe, you will not understand.

Keep the Faith!

John

References

Hannah Arendt, *The Life of the Mind: Willing*, one-volume edition (New York: Harvest/HBJ, 1978), 29, 30.

Frederick D. Wilhelmsen, *The Paradoxical Structure of Existence* (Dallas: The University of Dallas Press, 1970), 98, 114–15, 116–17.

Letter 11

Dear John,

Before I address any details of your latest, I am going to restate what I am arguing, since I fear we're in danger at times of ignoring the forest for the trees and getting lost in details.

You recall that a few letters ago, in order to restart the conversation, you suggested I might address how, as I see it, the crisis of modernity could most effectively be overcome. I pointed out in response that though the Church has been gradually but steadily losing her cultural standing in what was once Christendom since at least the sixteenth century, and arguably since about 1300, there was one period in which that trend seemed to be reversing, namely during the Catholic intellectual revival of the nineteenth and twentieth centuries. Obviously there were many ups and downs here, but it did seem to many, especially from about 1900 till sometime in the 1950s, that Catholicism had managed to regain some of its former cultural prestige. As I wrote a couple of letters ago, "There were numerous conversions of important intellectuals. Catholic thought was no longer ignored, but quite often given a respectful attention. Becoming a Catholic was now widely viewed as a perfectly legitimate, if still a bit daring, option." And I also noted that when Leo XIII took the already growing interest in the thought of St. Thomas and gave it the Church's official sanction, this gave an intellectual solidity to the revival. When Thomas began to be deemphasized in both philosophy and theology, when the clarity of doctrine that had been so marked an aspect of this movement began to blur, when it began to be felt that we Catholics somehow needed to model ourselves more after the world and its currents of thought—then the revival, already faltering a bit, totally collapsed. Now we're in the mess that we all recognize and that no one seems to know how to get out of. Given what has happened since the 1960s, inside as well as outside the Church, I'm far from sure that a revival of Thomism simply by itself would do much to extricate us from our current morass, but any successful strategy must, in my view, include a revived and vigorous Thomism.

But for you, it seems, Aquinas is not an antidote to modernity but its precursor. There is, you say, "a direct line between Thomas Aquinas and Isaac Newton." I think this judgment is mistaken, and moreover, I think that we must be careful to avoid a certain verbal confusion. When I quoted from Leo XIII's first encyclical, *Inscrutabili*, to the effect that it is philosophy "upon which the foundation of other sciences in great measure depends," you seem to have taken Leo to mean that when he spoke of the "*aliarum scientiarum ratio*," he meant science in the modern sense, especially as that term is used in the English-speaking world. But it's pretty clear that by *scientia* Leo did not have that in mind at all; he did not mean experimental physics or chemistry or biology, but rather science in the sense in which both philosophy and theology are sciences: Aristotle's knowledge through causes. If this is correct, then what Leo meant is clear. For theology itself does "in great measure" depend upon a right kind of philosophy. In *Pascendi* (no. 45) Pius X mandates that "scholastic philosophy be made the basis of the sacred sciences," and he means by "scholastic philosophy," as he points out immediately, "chiefly that which the Angelic Doctor has bequeathed to us." The reason why Leo and Pius wrote as they did will be clear if one considers what an unsound philosophy will do to theology. If someone bases his theology on, say, the philosophy of Kant, it will be distorted from the outset, since he will deny that we can meaningfully speak about God, except perhaps as an object of revelation. And from this we fall into a fideism, the blind alley into which so much of Protestant theology has fallen, being essentially unable to engage in intellectual communication with those who are not already converted. This is surely far from St. Paul's model of how to engage with nonbelievers when he spoke to the Areopagus in Athens (Acts 17). By doing this we are not reducing everything to reason, but simply pointing out that there are things which we, in common with the rest of mankind, naturally perceive, and we can make those things the basis of a shared discourse. Nor—to anticipate a possible objection—are those things we perceive in common primarily the stuff of science in the modern meaning of that word, nor are they limited to the bare phenomena that we can see or measure. For unless we hold to an empiricist position that we cannot go beyond what the senses grasp, human beings are able to reason from their observations to what lies beyond or behind them, as St. Paul so forcefully taught in Romans 1:19–20. Hence the whole domain of philosophy becomes something potentially shared with the rest of mankind.

You, however, are not comfortable with an assertion that Thomism must be the foundation for the Church's theological activity. You protest "the deification of Thomism, the reduction of the long history of Christian philosophy to one philosopher. . . . In truth, there is no 'Catholic' philosophy, there is only philosophy enlightened by Christianity, an enlightenment that will take many forms and follow many paths." I suspect, however, that your disagreement with me here goes much further than what you see as an illegitimate attempt to circumscribe Christian philosophy within one tradition. I suspect that you regard any claim that there is a best or most accurate tradition of philosophical thought as wrongheaded. Plato, Aristotle, Aquinas, Ockham, Descartes, Locke, Kant, Wittgenstein—all these and more are distinguished names in the history of philosophy, all offer insights and nothing but insights. Among all their methods and conclusions, we must simply pick and choose what we find helpful. But does not such an approach to philosophy trivialize it, make it simply an intellectual exercise or even a game, rather than an attempt, more or less successful, to arrive at truth by the use of reason? Moreover, ironically, is not such an approach dependent on, or at least redolent of, one particular philosophical school—the Kantian separation of the world of phenomena from the noumenal world—so that philosophers are doomed to argue incessantly about nothing more than their opinions, while reality itself forever eludes their intellectual grasp?

But while I do think that many things are accessible to our common human reason, not everything is. Thus there are things that are matters of revelation, which, for us, must be received by faith. I juxtaposed Hebrews 1:1 with Romans 1:19–20 to illustrate how this distinction is present in Sacred Scripture itself. I don't understand how you could think that I was saying that Hebrews 1:1 means that "the appearance of the Son makes things reducible to reason." I was only pointing out that the distinction between reason and faith was not something invented by Aquinas, but is present in the New Testament itself. "In many and various ways God spoke of old to our fathers by the prophets; but in these last days he has spoken to us by a Son. . . ."—what is this except an assertion of revelation, while Romans 1:19–20 is equally an assertion of the possibility of knowledge of God by the use of human reason? To eliminate either of these categories, either faith or reason, is fatal to both philosophy and theology, and indeed, to the entire tradition of salvation history as found in Scripture.

On another point of yours, I claimed that, speaking of philosophy, Thomas had sought to argue from first principles. You wrote, "Do you know of any philosopher who claims to start with secondary principles or to be aiming at error?" Well, yes, no doubt that's true, but I'm not clear as to your point. Philosophers *have* differed with each other, and no doubt each one believes he's correct and is starting from correctly perceived first principles. But the fact that each one thinks his own philosophy is right is hardly an argument against the possibility that someone *is* right. They can't all be right, to the extent that they differ. It's hardly unusual for someone to claim that the philosophical principles he adheres to are correct, whether he's a Kantian, a logical positivist, or whatever. Would you deny a Thomist the same right?

I may have misunderstood what you said about dialectics. I thought you probably meant by that the method of stating a question, raising objections, offering a response and then answering the objections, the method that Aquinas uses in the *Summa theologiae* and elsewhere. But not everywhere, especially not in his purely philosophical works, such as the *De principiis naturae* or the *De ente et essentia*. But perhaps by *dialectics* you meant simply the use of reason? If so, then I would hope that theology would always make use of reasonable argument, not in the sense that it begins from reasoning or from philosophy, but in the sense that it treats the data of revelation, the sources of revelation, reasonably. What other way of proceeding is there? Reason is not simply how our minds work, but more fundamentally and importantly, how reality, how being, *is*, since God himself is He Who Is.

Much of what you wrote about persons, about the uniqueness of each one of us, I will not argue with. But I will dispute the conclusions you draw from it. The fact that the advent of the Faith gave prominence to the individual and so eventually led (for example) to the abolition of slavery does not argue for the idea that "modern liberalism is the highest achievement of the Middle Ages." It only means that modernity or liberalism took over certain ideas which the Middle Ages had developed, and that, yes, the later Middle Ages were the beginnings of the transition to modernity. This, as I said in my last letter, was necessarily the case, since modernity was not something introduced from the outside, as if brought by space aliens.

Lastly, you bring up stories again. "For the truth about human reasoning," you wrote, "is that what a man considers 'reasonable' is dependent on what stories he carries around about the workings of the world." I don't deny the emotive power of stories. They seem to be what moves many people today. Hence, I agree that we need to highlight the Christian narrative, our entire story of salvation history, as a means of interesting people in the Faith. C. S. Lewis wrote that when he "read Chesterton's *Everlasting Man* and for the first time saw the whole Christian outline of history set out in a form that seemed to me to make sense," he "contrived not to be too badly shaken." But of course it was not then that Lewis converted, for an attractive story is not a *reason*. I see how a story could make one realize that something might be true, it might even make one wish that it were true. But in itself it does not constitute proof, does not give a reason. If it did, then maybe you and I could come up with a really attractive myth and start our own religion. We might even get lots of followers! After all, it's an old American pastime, indulged in by many from Joseph Smith to Mary Baker Eddy to Jim Jones.

Enough for now, John, and I look forward as usual to your reply.

Thomas

REFERENCE

C. S. Lewis, *Surprised by Joy*, chapter XIV.

Letter 12

Nisi Crederet,
Non Caperet

DEAR THOMAS,

I do not understand the distinction between "liberalism took over certain ideas which the Middle Ages had developed," and "liberalism is an achievement of the Middle Ages." I don't see how you can concede the former and deny the latter. The point is not trivial, since it determines how we shall approach the modern problem. By your scheme—which I think is the schema of all the *Traditionalists*—we should oppose it *simpliciter*; by mine, we should rescue it from its fundamental error (which also begins in the Middle Ages) and reconnect it with its religious roots. Those are two very different tasks.

And what is this fundamental error? It is the belief that there exists a purely *secular* space, divorced from the moral order. Now, this makes a certain degree of sense if one confines one's gaze to the physical parts of the cosmos. One need not, indeed cannot, allow moral considerations to color a computation of, say, the orbit of Venus or the refraction of light. And this "non-moral" view has proved powerful; for example, it allows us to have this conversation remotely, and even allows us, if we so choose, to continue this conversation over dinner tonight in Los Angeles or New York. However, I think this piecemeal vision fails when we turn our attention from the parts to the whole. When we look at the cosmos as a whole, we see order and beauty, and can understand them only through an aesthetic view. While the parts are governed by a strictly deterministic rationality, the whole is governed by order and beauty, which cannot be rationalized. The cosmos is cosmetic and not reducible to any strict rationality. Like all things cosmetic, it escapes the purely rational and invites contemplation. What it does not invite is some reduction of cosmic order to the four causes, the endpoint of all rational analysis; that is, the cosmos escapes rationalism.

I remember reading some scientist—I think it was Desmond Morris—explain "love" in terms of chemical reactions in the brain. And he is of course absolutely correct: viewing the beloved is reflected in chemical movements. He has therefore perfectly rationalized love, and completely missed it. And it is precisely here that we come up against the limits of rationalism: it is always a complete explanation that explains absolutely nothing; it gives (or can give) an exhaustive view of the parts and says nothing about the whole. Because the truth is that nothing important can be rationalized, not love, not the cosmos, not the Cross. This is not to say that these things are irrational, but it is to assert that they exceed the rational, overflow it, escape it. They cannot be reduced to their four causes.

This brings us to the very core of the difference between us, a difference that can neither be "split" by compromise nor synthesized by the dialectic. For you, and Leo, and for the modern "scientist," philosophy, and even natural philosophy (the older name for modern science) means, as you put it, "knowledge through causes," and specifically the four causes identified by Aristotle. But I assert, on the contrary, that nothing important has causes, and a "science" (modern or medieval) concerned only with causes will always miss the mark. *Things* have causes, *actions* have grounds; and it is with action, human or divine, that philosophy and theology are primarily concerned. "Causes" are deterministic (as in "cause and effect") and hence you cannot reduce the act of creation to its "causes," since to do so would deprive the creator of his (or His) freedom. Each created thing has causes, but being does not; it has only a ground, and the ground of being is love. I'm pretty sure you don't want to reduce that to some mixture of Aristotelian "causes."

At the very start of the modern era, the poet Angelus Silesius put it this way:

> *The rose is without why,*
> *She blooms because she blooms;*
> *She cares not for herself, cares not if she is seen.*

The rose can be "explained" by reduction to its four causes, but it cannot be understood in this way. The scientist or the rationalist philosopher can explain the rose only by ignoring its actual being. Not that this ignorance isn't a useful thing; were I in the rose market, understanding the causes would be of great help in growing more roses, and more beautiful roses. But it will never explain why people buy roses. As an action, the purchase does not have causes, but grounds. And one great difference between causes and grounds is that while the former is deterministic, the latter calls forth freedom: I can buy the rose or not; I can choose chocolate over roses, or choose nothing at all.

This concern with grounds rather than causes brings us immediately to the world of the artist and creator, for all things begin in art. It became popular in the high Middle Ages to present God as the Great Geometer; but in fact, he is the

Great Artist creating a cosmos, the root of "cosmetic," or perhaps the Great Potter, forming man out of the mud of the
earth. The geometer (*qua* geometer) creates nothing; the potter alone can say, "Behold, I am doing something new" (Isaiah
43:19).

It is interesting to note that the secular world depends on
the late medieval creation of a uniform, Cartesian notion of
space, one might almost say a "dead space." But the notion
does not begin with Descartes or with any scientist or philosopher, but with the artists, specifically Brunelleschi's demonstration of single-point perspective in 1420. This became the
standard for art, despite the fact that it was not realist at all,
and that is not the way people see things. For one thing, we
have two eyes rather than one, and our gaze is never fixed for
very long, and certainly not on an infinite "vanishing point,"
but is constantly changing. In reality, we are always dealing
with multiple perspectives, more like Van Eyck's *Ghent Altar-
piece* than Leon Alberti's explanation of Caravaggio's *Narcissus*
(the perfect symbol of his age, and ours). But the point is
that this secular space moved from art to science to philosophy, and not the other way round.

You say, "I suspect that you regard any claim that there is a
best or most accurate tradition of philosophical thought as
wrong-headed." While that is not entirely correct, neither is
it entirely wrong. Of course, if "science" is, as you say, the
resolution of things to their four causes, there can only be
one "right" answer and hence one right perspective, which
can be summarized by philosophy, of which there can only be
one "correct" version. I suspect this is what Leo had in mind,
and it certainly reflects any number of Thomists of my
acquaintance. Of course, once we have summarized this philosophy, it can be disseminated through the schools to pro-

duce an elite of right-thinking people, since it cannot be challenged intellectually. This, I think, is the dream both of the Thomists and of the modern cult of "expertise." (I can't help noticing how often the views of these two groups coincide in essence, even as they disagree on the particulars.) But this sounds to me like pure hubris. (I must admit here that this is not true of the post-modern Thomists, but that's another topic.)

But if we are, as I assert, more concerned with the grounds of human action as the object of philosophy (and all science), then another view emerges, because the same grounds can always lead to different actions. The grounds are given, but the responses are, or can be, free. And it is always impossible to say in advance whether a particular response is "correct," and it may not be possible to do so even in retrospect. But since God is the ultimate ground of all action, and since the infinity that is God, or rather the infinity that God exceeds, will never be captured by one philosophy, there can never be one "correct" philosophy; rather, each is a fragmentary view of the whole. Nor is this view especially at odds with Thomas, who hoped to synthesize contrary views into a consistent whole. That's an ambitious goal, and one which I think will be realized, but perhaps only in the last moment before the eschaton. Claims to have done so before then can legitimately be viewed with suspicion. In the meantime, we take multiple points of view and harmonize them only liturgically through praise.

But all of this is rooted not so much in bad philosophy as in bad anthropology. For the Thomist, like the capitalist, imagines man to be a "rational" machine. But "rational" here loses it connection with *ratio*, proportionality, to become something more like "calculating," either "utilities" (in the case of the capitalist) or "propositions" (in the case of the philosopher). But man does not work like that, and neither does God. Or at least, God chose to present himself as artist and historian rather than as philosopher. He gives us stories, not propositions. And the stories must be believed before they can be used. And he does this precisely because he is a better philosopher and a better psychologist. But he is also a better Father in that he always gives his children the best gifts possible. That being the case, I must start with the right stories rather than the "right" philosophy. Because that is how all people think and is the only way they can think.

Now, I know you would like to claim that you come to your beliefs "rationally," but I counter: you cannot possibly know that, since before you started your reflection on these things you were already laden with such an immense load of cultural baggage that it would be impossible to disentangle the "what I figured out for myself" from the "what I was given." Indeed, the pure "what I figured out for myself" cannot really be said to exist, since you can only figure thinks[†] out at all from what you have received previously. The truth is that we all carry around a "story" of how the world works, and this story filters all information we receive, categorizing each item as "credible" or not. You allow that stories have an "emotive" power but doubt their necessary hold on reason. But this gets it exactly backwards: a story *might* be emotive, but it *must* be reasonable. That is, a story *must be* proportional to a view of the world we either have or can imagine having. The story may extend or deepen our rationality, but it must

---

[†] A typo, I know, but I decided to keep it there and convert it into a Freudian slip. It seems to capture what I want to say.

appeal to it in some way, or else it will simply be rejected as untrue or uninteresting. And it is precisely this proportionality, this *ratio*, which constitutes reason itself. Indeed, in the light of Gödel's Incompleteness Theorem and Tarski's Undefinability Theorem, even mathematics and logic rest on a kernel of pure belief. Here I stand with Nicholas of Cusa to assert: *Nisi crederet, non caperet.*

Perhaps I did not express myself well, but you seem the think that I deny the distinction between faith and reason. I certainly do not, in fact I insist on it. What I do deny, in the most vehement terms possible, is the *opposition* between them asserted by Thomas, such that more of the one means less of the other. But I assert that there is never one without the other, and that the deepening of either leads to the extension of the other. The Beatific Vision will not be, as in Thomas, the end of faith, but its infinite deepening.

Finally ("At last," you say) let me close with a quotation from an Orthodox theologian, David Bentley Hart:

> Thus, for Christian thought, knowledge of the world is something to be achieved not just through a reconstruction of its "sufficient reason," but through an obedience to glory, an orientation of the will toward the light of being and its gratuity; and so the most fully "adequate" discourse of truth is worship, prayer, and rejoicing.
>
> Phrased otherwise, the truth of being is "poetic" before it is "rational" (indeed, it is rational precisely because of its supreme poetic coherence and richness of detail), and thus cannot be known truly if this order is reversed.
>
> Beauty is the beginning and end of all true knowledge: really to know, one must first love, and having

known, one must finally delight; only this "corresponds" to the Trinitarian love and delight that creates. The truth of being is the whole of being, in its event, groundless, and so, in its every detail, revelatory of the light that grants it.

All the best,
John

REFERENCE

David Bentley Hart, *The Hidden and the Manifest*, "The Offering of Names" (Grand Rapids: Eerdmans, 2017), 27.

Letter 13

Dear John,

For once you present me with an easy task at the outset! "I do not understand," you say, "the distinction between 'liberalism took over certain ideas which the Middle Ages had developed,' and 'liberalism is an achievement of the Middle Ages.'" But I don't think my point is all that arcane. The genealogy of ideas can take quite unexpected paths, and as the Middle Ages decayed, certain ideas developed which, when taken out of context or exaggerated, brought forth something new. Surely this sort of thing happens again and again in intellectual history. Augustine/Calvin, Luther/Thomas Müntzer, Hegel/Marx. But by "achievement" I understand something which is the logical culmination of something earlier, and I don't see that liberalism can be called an achievement of medieval thought, since it contradicts so much of that thought. You're familiar, I'm sure, with Alfred North Whitehead's remark that all of Western philosophy is a footnote to Plato. Yet would we want to call all that subsequent philosophical development an "achievement" of Plato, when most of it is in direct contradiction to Plato's own teaching? It developed out of Plato in the sense that one idea led to another, but not as anything rightly called an achievement of his.

But what about your next point? The "fundamental error" of modernity or liberalism, you say, is that "there exists a purely *secular* space, divorced from the moral order." Well, I myself think that there exists a space in which persons can talk with each other, though I would not call it either secular or "divorced from the moral order." It is simply the "space" in which we can meet and hold discourse. By a paradox, you appear to me to be the one who wants to create a space "divorced from the moral order," for you seem to think that any space in which those of differing views can meet and hold meaningful discourse is necessarily an empty space, a Cartesian space, a mechanistic space, such as the one that capitalism imagines the economy operates in. To explain further, let me hark back to something you wrote earlier (in the third letter):

> The modern world would have us believe that history is a science through which we can grasp the past with great certainty, but this is dubious. What happens is that the historian takes the fragments and assembles them into a story about the past. Or rather stories, because different historians tell different stories, each of which embodies a different understanding. So for example, we can know with precision when the Civil War began, but we can only argue about why it began. North and South tell a different story, and for each the history, the story they tell, enters into the realm of myth, a "truth" that endures, a "truth" that is their founding story, their enduring myth.

As I understand you here, it is *necessarily* futile to seek the truth about the causes of the Civil War. Not that it is difficult, not that there are so many persons and factors to consider that we will probably never have a completely satisfactory understanding, but that it is impossible in principle for those of different "tribes" to find agreement because each tells a different story. Apparently no hope here of these stories being corrected or refined by more research, by closer examination of contemporary opinion as contained, say, in diaries or letters, nothing but two opposing tribes, each with its own story, its own myths. But you do agree that these two tribes can reach agreement about comparatively trivial matters, such as when the war began, and so on. So in this space where discourse does occur, where we can agree on the date of the firing on Fort Sumter, can anything of importance occur? Am I not justified in calling it an empty space? It is the space, you say, in which science, of whatever sort, conducts its activities, the space in which we can know things that are measurable or dateable. But things of real importance cannot be addressed there.

At the end of the fifth letter you wrote,

> You want facts and I want faith; your faith is rooted in facts, my facts are rooted in faith. You want miracles that you might have faith; I want faith that I might see the miracles. And this faith arises from a story. This story is a history, but is not reachable by any historical method; it can only be accepted on faith alone. So there are no "mere stories"; there are only good and bad stories, better and worse stories.

So it is not only the truths of faith in the strict sense, such as the Trinity, but even the historical events upon which the Christian revelation depends, the Resurrection for example, that "cannot possibly be verified by any historical method," you say, for they constitute a "question beyond history." Such questions cannot be addressed in the space in which historians, and philosophers for that matter, work, in which they offer arguments and proofs accessible, in principle, to all. Does this not render such space void of all real content, meaningless as regards the truly important questions which mankind faces? If so, are we not then reduced to telling stories which contain our own worldviews, and which we hope that others will find attractive too?

If I understand your viewpoint correctly, does it not lead inexorably toward an inability to talk with anyone who is not already of your "tribe"? There is no common ground for anything of importance. But what do I think of this "space"? I think it is where we can indeed approach questions of meaning, a space by no means "divorced from the moral order," nor from the metaphysical order either. More than once in this exchange I have called your attention to Romans 1:19–21, where St. Paul notes that the existence of God, "his invisible nature, namely, his eternal power and deity, has been clearly perceived in the things that have been made." And one can find the same argumentation in the Book of Wisdom, chap. 13: "For all men who were ignorant of God were foolish by nature; and they were unable from the good things that are seen to know him who exists, nor did they recognize the craftsman while paying heed to his works." Here surely, in both the Old and New Testaments, is an acknowledgment of a common space in which all of mankind can recognize the existence of the unseen God by means of the visible world. A twofold sort of space, it seems to me. One, the literal space containing the "good things that are seen." The other, the intellectual space in which all of mankind can exercise its reasoning in and upon those good things. What do you make of this? How does it fit in with your (as far as I can see) claim that human beings can't get beyond the most basic empirical data within that space? "God chose to present himself as artist and historian rather than as philosopher. He gives us stories, not propositions," you state. Well, yes, there are a lot of stories in Sacred Scripture, but there are also these occasional assertions that certainly appear to be philosophical and have long been seen as such. So, really, what do you make of this? Are these not philosophical claims? They appear to apply to all of mankind, hearers of the most diverse stories anyone can imagine, with widely varying traditions, but still held accountable, according to Paul, because "although they knew God they did not honor him as God or give thanks to him."

To see God by means of the things that he has made is to make use of the idea of *causes*. I plead guilty to doing so. But what is wrong with this? "'Causes' are deterministic," you say. But are they always or necessarily so? Even we humans, rational creatures, act as efficient causes day in and day out, undetermined except to some kind of a perceived good. And still less is God, who created in entire freedom, determined.

I know that for over a hundred years it's been popular in Protestant theology to regard the use of philosophy in Christian thought as an alien importation of Hellenistic ideas into Christianity, and that since the Council such ideas have become popular even in some Catholic circles. "The thesis that the critically purified Greek heritage forms an integral part of Christian faith has been countered by the call for a de-Hellenization of Christianity—a call which has more and more dominated theological discussions since the beginning of the modern age," as Benedict XVI noted in his Regensburg address from 2006. And Benedict of course rejects such a movement, indeed calling St. Paul's vision in Acts 16 of the "man of Macedonia . . . beseeching him and saying, 'Come over to Macedonia and help us'" as a "'distillation' of the intrinsic necessity of a rapprochement between biblical faith and Greek inquiry." But if we accept that such a "rapprochement between biblical faith and Greek inquiry" does violence to neither, what becomes of your criticisms of rational argument as playing the role that I have been advocating?

Of course, I am not suggesting that reason can discover the truths of faith in the strict sense, but simply that the preambles of the Faith are accessible to reason. Since Catholicism is an historical religion, basing itself upon historical claims, naturally philosophy does not suffice to establish all of these preambles. So we have St. Paul in 1 Corinthians 15, referring to the "more than five hundred brethren" to whom the resurrected Christ appeared, acting as a sort of historian, citing his sources, calling up his witnesses, as it were. It appears to me that I have done nothing different from what the Church has been doing since her earliest days. If I am wrong in my approach, then it appears that the entire Church since the time of the Apostles has been wrong as well.

I reiterate: stories are fine, even necessary. For some they will be enough. But if the Church does not have much more; if she does not have the arguments that can show how mankind should have been able, "from the good things that are seen, to know him who exists"; if she is not able to appeal, as Paul did, to witnesses for the astounding fact of the Resurrection, then I don't understand how we're not in the same boat as any pagan religion which has plenty of fascinating stories, of great beauty even, but can advance no reasons as to why we should believe any of them.

All my best,
Thomas

REFERENCE

Benedict XVI, "Meeting with the Representatives of Science, Lecture of the Holy Father," Aula Magna of the University of Regensburg, 12 September 2006.

Letter 14

Space and Story and History

DEAR THOMAS,

I think the chief topic of your last was the relationship between faith and nature. You note the biblical admonitions in Paul and Wisdom to look at the natural world, and I would certainly not disagree with that. But then you make another move and imply that this look is "rationalistic." I do not see any grounds for this belief, and if you offered any, I missed it; it just seems to be an assumption (correct me if I got that wrong). For there is no chain of logic, beginning with whatever first principles you care to choose, that ends in the conclusion, "and then you place a lamb on the altar and kill it." This is simply not a "naturalistic" and certainly not a "philosophic" conclusion, and yet it is a conclusion that every culture reaches, in one form other another. But they do not reach it by philosophy. In fact, it is often the philosopher who calls that "naturalistic" conclusion into question.

Primitive man, and even not-so-primitive man, sees in nature a world imbued with life and spirit. It is a nature that will either care for him or kill him, and so it must be propitiated. He first does this with animal sacrifice, including the sacrifice of the animal known as "man," and then with a sacrifice of the things of the earth. This is in fact the first religious "argument" as recorded in the enmity between Cain and

127

Abel. Cain is the farmer offering the fruit of the soil, but when his sacrifice is not as pleasing as Abel's animal sacrifice, Cain goes him one better by sacrificing Abel. And thus, the history of the world begins. But where in this history do you see any trace of rationalism? You assert, "To see God by means of the things that he has made is to make use of the idea of causes. I plead guilty to doing so." That's a laudable philosophic position, but one that would have been unintelligible to most ages. When men saw the rainfall, they did not ask "What caused this?"; they asked, "Who caused this?" To most men in most times and places, the cosmos is personal. They were less interested in *how* the gods do what they do than in *why*—and mostly, how they could get these gods to do what we would like them to do.

And just as philosophy cannot reach the core of the faith, neither is there any rationality that reaches to the Cross, for it is not a "rational" act that could be deduced from first principles. It is an overflowing act of love expressed as pure self-sacrifice. And this sacrifice, rather than negating the pagan human sacrifices, perfects them, so much so that they no longer need to be offered; rather, the perfect human sacrifice is symbolically re-enacted each hour of the day in the form of bread and wine, the fruits of the soil. Cain and Abel are now reconciled. You cannot reduce these to any "four causes," for like being itself they have no cause. Love is the ground of being, not its cause; it is its reason, but never its rationale.

When man looks at nature, he sees the necessity of prayer, praise, and sacrifice. It is not until the philosopher comes along that he has grounds to doubt this. Philosophy always runs the risk of separating man from his most basic response to created beauty, a response rooted in awe and terror. As Hegel pointed out, this "alienation" is not entirely negative, since man can now be the object of his own reflection. But unless philosophy will itself be tamed by the original awe of nature, it runs the risk of trying to "tame" nature and thereby desacralizing it. And so it is today, in this age of the philosophers. It is a philosophy with the power to kill us all. The key word here is "tamed"; this is not to denigrate philosophy, but to recognize that, like fire, it is a useful tool and a terrible master. And unless it is "tamed," that is, relativized in relation to faith, it will become, indeed has become, our terrible master.

But the real issue is space, and here I find myself confused by your position. You say: "Well, I myself think that there exists a space in which persons can talk with each other, though I would not call it either secular or 'divorced from the moral order.' It is simply the 'space' in which we can meet and hold discourse." I am at a loss to see the difference between this "simply space" and Cartesian space. Of course, this Cartesian, "neutral" space is—or was—the foundation of modern physics and philosophy, but physics at least has had the good sense to abandon it. We now know that space is not uniform, but bends around objects; that is to say, space is constrained by what it contains, and the primary thing it contains is the cosmos, which shapes space to its own ends. You like the idea of a "neutral" space because you assert that's where dialogue can take place. Well, not in my experience, and I suspect not in yours. For dialogue always takes place in a cultural space, and is rooted in the cultural artifact known as "language," a distinguishing feature of being human. Are you really willing to assert that there exists some neutral cultural space that is "simply space"?

I think some are willing to assert this neutral space, and you might be among them: they believe that in pure logic we find the same neutrality as in pure mathematics. I am perfectly willing to concede that the relationships among the pure forms (numbers, circles, squares) take place in a neutral space, but only because it is no space at all, or at best an ethereal, platonic space; so long as there is no substantive content, there is no need of space, moral or neutral.

But in the world of men, we are shaped by culture, language, economics, and belief. And each of these cultures embodies its own "logic" which will generally be unintelligible to those outside the culture, unless and until they make an effort to enter the culture, or at least to learn the language. Now, cultures tend to overlap with one another, and in these shared spaces a dialogue can take place. But no tradition accepts an outside critique. That does not mean that the tradition is static and self-perpetuating, for questions arise internally over different interpretations of its texts and rites, or by facing new situations to which the texts must be applied. If the tradition is to survive, it must summon the resources to overcome these difficulties and will do so by developing theories and methods of problem resolution. However, it is inevitable that a tradition will come against problems which cannot be overcome by its internal resources and this leads to an epistemological crisis. The tradition can only overcome this crisis by opening itself to other and rival traditions, by learning to speak "a second first language," as Alasdair MacIntyre puts it. The only alternative is defeat and death. Christians learned early on that they would have to learn to "speak Greek" in order to handle all the problems posed by the revelation of Christ. But nowhere did they think that speaking Greek would relativize faith; that was a later delusion, and one that has led to the situation we have.

I gather that you would like to place history in this neutral space occupied by logic and mathematics. The odd thing is that I doubt you could find a single historian who would agree with that. You might have been able to do so in the nineteenth century, when the humane sciences attempted to ape the physical sciences in a frenzy of what one wit called "physics envy," but I don't think any historian is that "scientific" today. For what you are refusing is the distinction referred to earlier, the distinction between a "fact" and a "judgment." It is a fact that the bombardment of Fort Sumter began on April 12, 1861; it is a judgment as to why that bombardment began. Historians can determine facts with greater or lesser degrees of certitude; but they can only inform our judgments. Never will you hear an historian make a statement in the form, "The Civil War was caused 42.8% by slavery, 31.5% by states' rights, 6.8% by tariffs...," etc. The facts enrich our judgments, but these judgments are always subject to review and revision, save in the most trivial of matters. In recounting the history, some will emphasize slavery as the "cause," others the fear of the rise of a totalizing nation-state ruled from Washington. Neither judgment is entirely wrong, but some judgments are better than others, better because they cover more of the grounds and cover more of the facts. But of one judgment I am certain: history can never be "knowledge by causes," can never reduce any event to its supposed four causes, for these facts, like all human actions, don't have "causes," but "grounds," another distinction you have refused. No, it is not *futile* to discuss the causes of the Civil War, but it is arrogant to think one has the true and only description of those causes, for here we pass into the world of judgments.

Nor do I think that you want what you wish for. You want

the supernatural event of the Resurrection judged as "historical," and without reference to faith. But the best the historian can say is that some people believed they saw a dead man walking. As to whether they saw what they thought they did, they cannot say; it is simply beyond the domain of their science. Nor do I wish for them to say this. Do you really want the truths of religion subject to the jury of the historians? I don't.

But the really great paradox is that you simultaneously reject liberalism as the achievement of patristic and medieval Christianity, while accepting the very point upon which the secularization of that liberalism was accomplished: the existence of a neutral, "secular" space. What you are really pushing is Enlightenment rationalism, the neutral "marketplace of ideas," in which all have a say and the best man wins. It is an academic edition of market capitalism. By moving the debate to this supposedly "neutral" space, you have moved it to the enemy's own ground. That space is not "neutral" as advertised, but is occupied territory, chock full of all the values of modernity; if you choose to fight your battle there, they will take you front, flank, and rear. In fact (or maybe this is a judgment) that's pretty much the fate of the Christian rationalist as we actually see it.

So, we finally return to the question of stories versus... Well, what, exactly? What is on the other side? Is it really logic? Surely you are not trying to rationalize revelation. You are willing to concede, albeit weakly, that, "Well, yes, there are a lot of stories in Sacred Scripture," but that's the end of your commentary on the subject. You then assert, "but there are also these occasional assertions that certainly appear to be philosophical and have long been seen as such." Well, I suppose if you define philosophy broadly enough, there are philosophical statements, but as for there being a rigorous inquiry into four causes or the ultimate nature of being, and the like, I don't see it. Perhaps I have overlooked something, so if you can find a passage that meets any philosopher's definition of rigorous inquiry, I would like to hear it. If you merely mean statements that have philosophic implications, then that's all language; "Never wear white after Labor Day" assumes a whole set of social and normative relationships. It might be philosophic, but I wouldn't class it as a philosophic inquiry. The Gospels are just not interested in that. Philosophy as a reflection on the gospel is fine, but as the point of the gospel, well, there I must dissent.

So I return to my question: Why does God, who always gives us the best gifts possible, choose to speak to us in stories rather than in *Summas*? I gather that you think that if the Resurrection can be demonstrated to be "historical" then everybody will have to believe. But the reverse is true: unless they believe, they cannot accept the story as historical. You cannot reduce the Resurrection to knowledge by causes, nor can love be contained within logic, for love creates its own logic and supplies its own ground. It bends all space to its movement, and draws all men to itself.

Regards,
John

Letter 15

Dear John,

I think this is a good point at which to wrap up our discussion—you've just restated some of your main points and tied the whole conversation nicely together. Both of us will admit that we're still far apart on certain points.

In my last letter I made reference to two passages from Holy Scripture, Romans 1:19–21 and Wisdom 13:1. You responded by saying that I had called attention to "the biblical admonitions in Paul and Wisdom to look at the natural world." But no, not the natural world. The text from Wisdom reproves those who are unable or unwilling to go beyond "the good things that are seen" to the Something, or rather Someone, beyond the natural world, namely, God. Although there are certainly passages in Scripture that look upon God's creation with wonder and joy (e.g., Psalm 148 and Daniel 3:57–81), the two passages I called attention to (Romans and Wisdom) call upon us to look at the natural world only in order to know God, because God is knowable in part through his works. I said that these two passages contained a philosophical argument, an argument, to be sure, not stated with the precision that it later came to have, but sufficiently clear, and sufficiently philosophical. And it offers evidence that from the beginning (indeed, even under the Old Law) the Church was aware of and approved of an approach to God, a justification for his existence, that did not depend on prior faith, that in principle was open to all reasoning minds. As Maritain wrote,

Before entering into the sphere of completely formed
and articulated knowledge, in particular the sphere of
metaphysical knowledge, the human mind is indeed
capable of a prephilosophical knowledge which is *virtually metaphysical*. Therein is found the first, the primor-
dial way of approach through which men become
aware of the existence of God.

This prephilosophical knowledge seems to be native to the
human race, for the almost universal recognition that there
are powers beyond nature depends on some such "virtually
metaphysical" inference. At all events, it is assumed by Holy
Scripture to offer a means of access to God.

But this way of approaching God has not impressed you.
"Hymns to the pure ideas are rather rare, and liturgies that
invoke the *primum mobile* are not well attended," you wrote at
the very outset of our exchange. You point out that the
human religious instinct is something different, not something derived from any philosophical argument. And it is
true, as you said, that man's deep-rooted instinct to offer sacrifice to Divinity did not arise from any philosophical argument and is strictly speaking something apart from such an
argument.

This instinct to sacrifice to which you've rightly called
attention more than once—where did that come from? "For
there is no chain of logic, beginning with whatever first principles you care to choose, that ends in the conclusion, 'and
then you place a lamb on the altar and kill it.'" True, and
nicely put, by the way. This human instinct to propitiate the
powers beyond nature by a sacrifice seems, as far as I can see,
to have been one of the most profound results of the Fall, of
man's revolting against God, of man's inherited feelings of
guilt for doing so. Not a strictly philosophical conclusion,

perhaps, but still, a not unreasonable response on the part of humanity to our obscure perception or intuition that things are not quite right between us and whatever divine powers exist. As Aquinas noted:

> Natural reason tells man that he is subject to a higher being, on account of the defects which he perceives in himself, and in which he needs help and direction from someone above him. . . . Now just as in natural things the lower are naturally subject to the higher, so too it is a dictate of natural reason in accordance with man's natural inclination that he should tender submission and honor, according to his mode, to that which is above man. . . . Hence it is a dictate of natural reason that man should use certain sensibles, by offering them to God in sign of the subjection and honor due to Him. . . . Now this is what we mean by sacrifice, and consequently the offering of sacrifice is of the natural law.

This nearly omnipresent human practice of offering sacrifice is indeed a powerful argument that must be stressed, but in itself it doesn't prove the existence of the Being to whom sacrifice ultimately is offered. But neither the near ubiquity of sacrifice nor the sort of reasoning that Paul and the author of Wisdom set forth on behalf of a natural knowledge of God need be taken in isolation from each other—let alone opposed to each other—and a well-constructed apologetics or philosophy of religion will not do so.

Another chief point at issue between us has been that of "space," that is, of an intellectual space in which discourse may be conducted. You insist that this space must be Cartesian or the space of Newtonian physics. I don't see why. I can't help thinking that by privileging stories, as you do, you've made it, in principle, impossible for people of different cultures or religions to talk to each other. Each one has a story, and I can't figure out, on your view, how we are to know which story to accept. The one that is more "comprehensive," you reply. But surely that is about as subjective a standard as one could appeal to. A Muslim, I'd think, could claim that his story of salvation history was more comprehensive than the Christian because his incorporates both the Jewish and Christian stories but adds something additional. And Bahá'ís could claim to be even more comprehensive, as they add Krishna and Zoroaster to the above, as well as their own proper claimant to a divine revelation. I don't see that this is a fruitful way to proceed.

Our discussion of stories has always been related to the question of history. And your attitude toward history and historical testimony has been troubling to me from the outset. You wrote that

> if you are going to accept the Resurrection as an historical reality independent of the beliefs of the observer and base this "reality" solely on the testimony of the Christian witnesses, then you are going to have to accept the historicity of the Book of Mormon or the appearance of Gabriel to Muhammad on the same grounds. . . .

When St. Paul appealed to those who had seen the Risen Christ in 1 Corinthians 15, was he not appealing to "the testimony of the Christian witnesses"? I will not belabor this point here, as I've dealt with it in some of my earlier letters. But for a religion, such as the Catholic Faith, that stands or falls based upon the truth of certain historical claims, how in the world are we to hold fast to this Faith if we think those historical claims are no more probable than any other (and presumably discredited) narratives? As Etienne Gilson wrote: "No man would ever admit that God has spoken, unless he had solid proofs of the fact. Such proofs are to be found in history, where the miracles of God . . . prove His presence, the truth of His doctrine and the permanence of His inspiration."

In the 1907 decree of the Holy Office, *Lamentabili*, one of the condemned propositions, no. 36, runs in part: "The Resurrection of the Savior is not properly a fact of the historical order. It is a fact of merely the supernatural order (neither demonstrated nor demonstrable). . . ." Now I'm not accusing you of holding that condemned proposition, but I do think that your argument tends to lead in that direction. Since, as you appear to think, the Resurrection is simply something one embraces by faith, and the witnesses are by necessity no more reliable than Joseph Smith's cronies, is it not a small step to begin thinking that it is "not properly a fact of the historical order," and hence is "neither demonstrated nor demonstrable"?

There are historical facts that *can* be known by historical evidence, you say. For example, the date of the firing on Fort Sumter. As to anything more significant, such as the causes of the war, all we have are differing and competing stories: "So for example, we can know with precision when the Civil War began, but we can only argue about why it began. North and South tell a different story, and for each the history, the story they tell, enters into the realm of myth. . . ." But what in the world will these historians argue about if it's just a matter of telling stories? Can historians never argue *rationally* about causes, about why such and such an event occurred? Can there never be better and worse arguments, better and worse evidence? This is not to deny that sometimes there may be subjective factors in evaluating evidence, but that's a far cry from saying all we can do is trade stories.

I never claimed that we could know with exactitude the weight which we should give to each factor as a cause for the war: slavery, cultural differences between the two regions, states' rights, etc. But I do claim that we can do more than simply tell different stories. We can engage in a dialogue, we can point out insufficient or untrustworthy evidence as well as bad arguments, we can, in short, make use of a shared space in which discourse is possible, and can even be fruitful. Fr. Sokolowski's remarks on phenomenology may be given a wider significance here and applied to all human attempts at argument: "If we do not have a world in common, then we do not enter into a life of reason, evidence, and truth. Each of us turns to his own private world, and in the practical order we do our own thing: the truth does not make any demands on us."

The Church today certainly faces difficulties, not only in her work of evangelizing but even in keeping her own members faithful. I said before that I'm not opposed to making use of many and various methods. Indeed, it is imperative that, as part of our catechesis and apologetic, we present salvation history as the story that it is. Certainly it is compelling simply as story. I only insist that we must also present the kinds of public arguments that we used to call the preambles of the Faith—at the very least we have to keep them in reserve for those who ask for them, who ask for "a reason for the hope that is in [us]." Otherwise, what do we have? Your story and mine, his story and hers, their story and ours, but none ever based on anything save the shifting sands of personal taste or subjective attraction.

All the best always,
Thomas

REFERENCES

Etienne Gilson, *Reason and Revelation in the Middle Ages* (New York: Charles Scribner's, 1938), 81–82.

Jacques Maritain, *Approaches to God*, chapter 1.

Robert Sokolowski, *Introduction to Phenomenology* (Cambridge: Cambridge University Press, 2000), 10.

Thomas Aquinas, *Summa theologiae* II-II, q. 85, art. 1. See also III, q. 48, art. 3.

Appendix

Plato's *Euthyphro*[†]

Persons of the Dialogue: Socrates, Euthyphro.
Scene:The Porch of the King Archon.

EUTHYPHRO: Why have you left the Lyceum, Socrates? and what are you doing in the Porch of the King Archon? Surely you cannot be concerned in a suit before the King, like myself?

SOCRATES: Not in a suit, Euthyphro; impeachment is the word which the Athenians use.

EUTHYPHRO: What! I suppose that some one has been prosecuting you, for I cannot believe that you are the prosecutor of another.

SOCRATES: Certainly not.

EUTHYPHRO: Then some one else has been prosecuting you?

SOCRATES: Yes.

EUTHYPHRO: And who is he?

SOCRATES: A young man who is little known, Euthyphro; and I hardly know him: his name is Meletus, and he is of the deme of Pitthis. Perhaps you may remember his appearance; he has a beak, and long straight hair, and a beard which is ill grown.

[†] Translated by Benjamin Jowett. Text from eBooks@Adelaide, The University of Adelaide Library, South Australia.

EUTHYPHRO: No, I do not remember him, Socrates. But what is the charge which he brings against you?

SOCRATES: What is the charge? Well, a very serious charge, which shows a good deal of character in the young man, and for which he is certainly not to be despised. He says he knows how the youth are corrupted and who are their corruptors. I fancy that he must be a wise man, and see-ing that I am the reverse of a wise man, he has found me out, and is going to accuse me of corrupting his young friends. And of this our mother the state is to be the judge. Of all our political men he is the only one who seems to me to begin in the right way, with the cultivation of virtue in youth; like a good husbandman, he makes the young shoots his first care, and clears away us who are the destroyers of them. This is only the first step; he will afterwards attend to the elder branches; and if he goes on as he has begun, he will be a very great public benefactor.

EUTHYPHRO: I hope that he may; but I rather fear, Socrates, that the opposite will turn out to be the truth. My opinion is that in attacking you he is simply aiming a blow at the foundation of the state. But in what way does he say that you corrupt the young?

SOCRATES: He brings a wonderful accusation against me, which at first hearing excites surprise: he says that I am a poet or maker of gods, and that I invent new gods and deny the existence of old ones; this is the ground of his indict-ment.

EUTHYPHRO: I understand, Socrates; he means to attack you about the familiar sign which occasionally, as you say, comes to you. He thinks that you are a neologian, and he is going to have you up before the court for this. He knows that such a charge is readily received by the world, as I myself know too well; for when I speak in the assembly about divine things, and foretell the future to them, they laugh at me and think me a madman. Yet every word that I say is true. But they are jealous of us all; and we must be brave and go at them.

SOCRATES: Their laughter, friend Euthyphro, is not a matter of much consequence. For a man may be thought wise; but the Athenians, I suspect, do not much trouble themselves about him until he begins to impart his wisdom to others, and then for some reason or other, perhaps, as you say, from jealousy, they are angry.

EUTHYPHRO: I am never likely to try their temper in this way.

SOCRATES: I dare say not, for you are reserved in your behaviour, and seldom impart your wisdom. But I have a benevolent habit of pouring out myself to everybody, and would even pay for a listener, and I am afraid that the Athenians may think me too talkative. Now if, as I was saying, they would only laugh at me, as you say that they laugh at you, the time might pass gaily enough in the court; but perhaps they may be in earnest, and then what the end will be you soothsayers only can predict.

EUTHYPHRO: I dare say that the affair will end in nothing, Socrates, and that you will win your cause; and I think that I shall win my own.

SOCRATES: And what is your suit, Euthyphro? are you the pursuer or the defendant?

EUTHYPHRO: I am the pursuer.

SOCRATES: Of whom?

EUTHYPHRO: You will think me mad when I tell you.

SOCRATES: Why, has the fugitive wings?

EUTHYPHRO: Nay, he is not very volatile at his time of life.

145

SOCRATES: Who is he?

EUTHYPHRO: My father.

SOCRATES: Your father! my good man?

EUTHYPHRO: Yes.

SOCRATES: And of what is he accused?

EUTHYPHRO: Of murder, Socrates.

SOCRATES: By the powers, Euthyphro! how little does the common herd know of the nature of right and truth. A man must be an extraordinary man, and have made great strides in wisdom, before he could have seen his way to bring such an action.

EUTHYPHRO: Indeed, Socrates, he must.

SOCRATES: I suppose that the man whom your father murdered was one of your relatives—clearly he was; for if he had been a stranger you would never have thought of prosecuting him.

EUTHYPHRO: I am amused, Socrates, at your making a distinction between one who is a relation and one who is not a relation; for surely the pollution is the same in either case, if you knowingly associate with the murderer when you ought to clear yourself and him by proceeding against him. The real question is whether the murdered man has been justly slain. If justly, then your duty is to let the matter alone; but if unjustly, then even if the murderer lives under the same roof with you and eats at the same table, proceed against him. Now the man who is dead was a poor dependant of mine who worked for us as a field labourer on our farm in Naxos, and one day in a fit of drunken passion he got into a quarrel with one of our domestic servants and slew him. My father bound him hand and foot and threw him into a ditch, and then sent to Athens to ask of a diviner what he should do with him. Meanwhile he never attended to him and took no care about him, for he regarded him as a murderer; and thought that no great harm would be done even if he did die. Now this was just what happened. For such was the effect of cold and hunger and chains upon him, that before the messenger returned from the diviner, he was dead. And my father and family are angry with me for taking the part of the murderer and prosecuting my father. They say that he did not kill him, and that if he did, the dead man was but a murderer, and I ought not to take any notice, for that a son is impious who prosecutes a father. Which shows, Socrates, how little they know what the gods think about piety and impiety.

SOCRATES: Good heavens, Euthyphro! and is your knowledge of religion and of things pious and impious so very exact, that, supposing the circumstances to be as you state them, you are not afraid lest you too may be doing an impious thing in bringing an action against your father?

EUTHYPHRO: The best of Euthyphro, and that which distinguishes him, Socrates, from other men, is his exact knowledge of all such matters. What should I be good for without it?

SOCRATES: Rare friend! I think that I cannot do better than be your disciple. Then before the trial with Meletus comes on I shall challenge him, and say that I have always had a great interest in religious questions, and now, as he charges me with rash imaginations and innovations in religion, I have become your disciple. You, Meletus, as I shall say to him, acknowledge Euthyphro to be a great theologian, and sound in his opinions; and if you approve of him you ought to approve of me, and not have me into court; but if you disapprove, you should begin by indicting him who is my teacher, and who will be the ruin, not of the young, but of the old;

that is to say, of myself whom he instructs, and of his old father whom he admonishes and chastises. And if Meletus refuses to listen to me, but will go on, and will not shift the indictment from me to you, I cannot do better than repeat this challenge in the court.

EUTHYPHRO: Yes, indeed, Socrates; and if he attempts to indict me I am mistaken if I do not find a flaw in him; the court shall have a great deal more to say to him than to me.

SOCRATES: And I, my dear friend, knowing this, am desirous of becoming your disciple. For I observe that no one appears to notice you—not even this Meletus; but his sharp eyes have found me out at once, and he has indicted me for impiety. And therefore, I adjure you to tell me the nature of piety and impiety, which you said that you knew so well, and of murder, and of other offences against the gods. What are they? Is not piety in every action always the same? and impiety, again—is it not always the opposite of piety, and also the same with itself, having, as impiety, one notion which includes whatever is impious?

EUTHYPHRO: To be sure, Socrates.

SOCRATES: And what is piety, and what is impiety?

EUTHYPHRO: Piety is doing as I am doing; that is to say, prosecuting any one who is guilty of murder, sacrilege, or of any similar crime—whether he be your father or mother, or whoever he may be—that makes no difference; and not to prosecute them is impiety. And please to consider, Socrates, what a notable proof I will give you of the truth of my words, a proof which I have already given to others:—of the principle, I mean, that the impious, whoever he may be, ought not to go unpunished. For do not men regard Zeus as the best and most righteous of the gods?—and yet they admit that he bound his father (Cronos) because he wickedly devoured his sons, and that he too had punished his own father (Uranus) for a similar reason, in a nameless manner. And yet when I proceed against my father, they are angry with me. So inconsistent are they in their way of talking when the gods are concerned, and when I am concerned.

SOCRATES: May not this be the reason, Euthyphro, why I am charged with impiety—that I cannot away with these stories about the gods? and therefore I suppose that people think me wrong. But, as you who are well informed about them approve of them, I cannot do better than assent to your superior wisdom. What else can I say, confessing as I do, that I know nothing about them? Tell me, for the love of Zeus, whether you really believe that they are true.

EUTHYPHRO: Yes, Socrates; and things more wonderful still, of which the world is in ignorance.

SOCRATES: And do you really believe that the gods fought with one another, and had dire quarrels, battles, and the like, as the poets say, and as you may see represented in the works of great artists? The temples are full of them; and notably the robe of Athene, which is carried up to the Acropolis at the great Panathenaea, is embroidered with them. Are all these tales of the gods true, Euthyphro?

EUTHYPHRO: Yes, Socrates; and, as I was saying, I can tell you, if you would like to hear them, many other things about the gods which would quite amaze you.

SOCRATES: I dare say; and you shall tell me them at some other time when I have leisure. But just at present I would rather hear from you a more precise answer, which you have not as yet given, my friend, to the question, What is "piety"? When asked, you only replied, Doing as you do, charging your father with murder.

EUTHYPHRO: And what I said was true, Socrates.

SOCRATES: No doubt, Euthyphro; but you would admit that there are many other pious acts?

EUTHYPHRO: There are.

SOCRATES: Remember that I did not ask you to give me two or three examples of piety, but to explain the general idea which makes all pious things to be pious. Do you not recollect that there was one idea which made the impious impious, and the pious pious?

EUTHYPHRO: I remember.

SOCRATES: Tell me what is the nature of this idea, and then I shall have a standard to which I may look, and by which I may measure actions, whether yours or those of any one else, and then I shall be able to say that such and such an action is pious, such another impious.

EUTHYPHRO: I will tell you, if you like.

SOCRATES: I should very much like.

EUTHYPHRO: Piety, then, is that which is dear to the gods, and impiety is that which is not dear to them.

SOCRATES: Very good, Euthyphro; you have now given me the sort of answer which I wanted. But whether what you say is true or not I cannot as yet tell, although I make no doubt that you will prove the truth of your words.

EUTHYPHRO: Of course.

SOCRATES: Come, then, and let us examine what we are saying. That thing or person which is dear to the gods is pious, and that thing or person which is hateful to the gods is impious, these two being the extreme opposites of one another. Was not that said?

EUTHYPHRO: It was.

SOCRATES: And well said?

EUTHYPHRO: Yes, Socrates, I thought so; it was certainly said.

SOCRATES: And further, Euthyphro, the gods were admitted to have enmities and hatreds and differences?

EUTHYPHRO: Yes, that was also said.

SOCRATES: And what sort of difference creates enmity and anger? Suppose for example that you and I, my good friend, differ about a number; do differences of this sort make us enemies and set us at variance with one another? Do we not go at once to arithmetic, and put an end to them by a sum?

EUTHYPHRO: True.

SOCRATES: Or suppose that we differ about magnitudes, do we not quickly end the differences by measuring?

EUTHYPHRO: Very true.

SOCRATES: And we end a controversy about heavy and light by resorting to a weighing machine?

EUTHYPHRO: To be sure.

SOCRATES: But what differences are there which cannot be thus decided, and which therefore make us angry and set us at enmity with one another? I dare say the answer does not occur to you at the moment, and therefore I will suggest that these enmities arise when the matters of difference are the just and unjust, good and evil, honourable and dishonourable. Are not these the points about which men differ, and about which when we are unable satisfactorily to decide our differences, you and I and all of us quarrel, when we do quarrel?

EUTHYPHRO: Yes, Socrates, the nature of the differences about which we quarrel is such as you describe.

SOCRATES: And the quarrels of the gods, noble Euthyphro, when they occur, are of a like nature?

EUTHYPHRO: Certainly they are.

SOCRATES: They have differences of opinion, as you say,

about good and evil, just and unjust, honourable and dishonourable: there would have been no quarrels among them, if
there had been no such differences—would there now?

EUTHYPHRO: You are quite right.

SOCRATES: Does not every man love that which he
deems noble and just and good, and hate the opposite of
them?

EUTHYPHRO: Very true.

SOCRATES: But, as you say, people regard the same
things, some as just and others as unjust—about these they
dispute; and so there arise wars and fightings among them.

EUTHYPHRO: Very true.

SOCRATES: Then the same things are hated by the gods
and loved by the gods, and are both hateful and dear to them?

EUTHYPHRO: True.

SOCRATES: And upon this view the same things, Euthyphro, will be pious and also impious?

EUTHYPHRO: So I should suppose.

SOCRATES: Then, my friend, I remark with surprise that
you have not answered the question which I asked. For I certainly did not ask you to tell me what action is both pious and
impious: but now it would seem that what is loved by the
gods is also hated by them. And therefore, Euthyphro, in thus
chastising your father you may very likely be doing what is
agreeable to Zeus but disagreeable to Cronos or Uranus, and
what is acceptable to Hephaestus but unacceptable to Here,
and there may be other gods who have similar differences of
opinion.

EUTHYPHRO: But I believe, Socrates, that all the gods
would be agreed as to the propriety of punishing a murderer:
there would be no difference of opinion about that.

SOCRATES: Well, but speaking of men, Euthyphro, did

Appendix

you ever hear any one arguing that a murderer or any sort of evil-doer ought to be let off?

EUTHYPHRO: I should rather say that these are the questions which they are always arguing, especially in courts of law: they commit all sorts of crimes, and there is nothing which they will not do or say in their own defence.

SOCRATES: But do they admit their guilt, Euthyphro, and yet say that they ought not to be punished?

EUTHYPHRO: No; they do not.

SOCRATES: Then there are some things which they do not venture to say and do: for they do not venture to argue that the guilty are to be unpunished, but they deny their guilt, do they not?

EUTHYPHRO: Yes.

SOCRATES: Then they do not argue that the evil-doer should not be punished, but they argue about the fact of who the evil-doer is, and what he did and when?

EUTHYPHRO: True.

SOCRATES: And the gods are in the same case, if as you assert they quarrel about just and unjust, and some of them say while others deny that injustice is done among them. For surely neither God nor man will ever venture to say that the doer of injustice is not to be punished?

EUTHYPHRO: That is true, Socrates, in the main.

SOCRATES: But they join issue about the particulars— gods and men alike; and, if they dispute at all, they dispute about some act which is called in question, and which by some is affirmed to be just, by others to be unjust. Is not that true?

EUTHYPHRO: Quite true.

SOCRATES: Well then, my dear friend Euthyphro, do tell me, for my better instruction and information, what proof have you that in the opinion of all the gods a servant who is guilty of murder, and is put in chains by the master of the dead man, and dies because he is put in chains before he who bound him can learn from the interpreters of the gods what he ought to do with him, dies unjustly; and that on behalf of such an one a son ought to proceed against his father and accuse him of murder. How would you show that all the gods absolutely agree in approving of his act? Prove to me that they do, and I will applaud your wisdom as long as I live.

EUTHYPHRO: It will be a difficult task; but I could make the matter very clear indeed to you.

SOCRATES: I understand; you mean to say that I am not so quick of apprehension as the judges: for to them you will be sure to prove that the act is unjust, and hateful to the gods.

EUTHYPHRO: Yes indeed, Socrates; at least if they will listen to me.

SOCRATES: But they will be sure to listen if they find that you are a good speaker. There was a notion that came into my mind while you were speaking; I said to myself: "Well, and what if Euthyphro does prove to me that all the gods regarded the death of the serf as unjust, how do I know anything more of the nature of piety and impiety? for granting that this action may be hateful to the gods, still piety and impiety are not adequately defined by these distinctions, for that which is hateful to the gods has been shown to be also pleasing and dear to them." And therefore, Euthyphro, I do not ask you to prove this; I will suppose, if you like, that all the gods condemn and abominate such an action. But I will amend the definition so far as to say that what all the gods hate is impious, and what they love pious or holy; and what some of them love and others hate is both or neither. Shall this be our definition of piety and impiety?

EUTHYPHRO: Why not, Socrates?

SOCRATES: Why not! certainly, as far as I am concerned, Euthyphro, there is no reason why not. But whether this admission will greatly assist you in the task of instructing me as you promised, is a matter for you to consider.

EUTHYPHRO: Yes, I should say that what all the gods love is pious and holy, and the opposite which they all hate, impious.

SOCRATES: Ought we to enquire into the truth of this, Euthyphro, or simply to accept the mere statement on our own authority and that of others? What do you say?

EUTHYPHRO: We should enquire; and I believe that the statement will stand the test of enquiry.

SOCRATES: We shall know better, my good friend, in a little while. The point which I should first wish to understand is whether the pious or holy is beloved by the gods because it is holy, or holy because it is beloved of the gods.

EUTHYPHRO: I do not understand your meaning, Socrates.

SOCRATES: I will endeavour to explain: we speak of carrying and we speak of being carried, of leading and being led, seeing and being seen. You know that in all such cases there is a difference, and you know also in what the difference lies?

EUTHYPHRO: I think that I understand.

SOCRATES: And is not that which is beloved distinct from that which loves?

EUTHYPHRO: Certainly.

SOCRATES: Well; and now tell me, is that which is carried in this state of carrying because it is carried, or for some other reason?

EUTHYPHRO: No; that is the reason.

SOCRATES: And the same is true of what is led and of what is seen?

EUTHYPHRO: True.

SOCRATES: And a thing is not seen because it is visible, but conversely, visible because it is seen; nor is a thing led because it is in the state of being led, or carried because it is in the state of being carried, but the converse of this. And now I think, Euthyphro, that my meaning will be intelligible; and my meaning is, that any state of action or passion implies previous action or passion. It does not become because it is becoming, but it is in a state of becoming because it becomes; neither does it suffer because it is in a state of suffering, but it is in a state of suffering because it suffers. Do you not agree?

EUTHYPHRO: Yes.

SOCRATES: Is not that which is loved in some state either of becoming or suffering?

EUTHYPHRO: Yes.

SOCRATES: And the same holds as in the previous instances; the state of being loved follows the act of being loved, and not the act the state.

EUTHYPHRO: Certainly.

SOCRATES: And what do you say of piety, Euthyphro: is not piety, according to your definition, loved by all the gods?

EUTHYPHRO: Yes.

SOCRATES: Because it is pious or holy, or for some other reason?

EUTHYPHRO: No, that is the reason.

SOCRATES: It is loved because it is holy, not holy because it is loved?

EUTHYPHRO: Yes.

SOCRATES: And that which is dear to the gods is loved by them, and is in a state to be loved of them because it is loved of them?

EUTHYPHRO: Certainly.

SOCRATES: Then that which is dear to the gods, Euthyphro, is not holy, nor is that which is holy loved of God, as you affirm; but they are two different things.

EUTHYPHRO: How do you mean, Socrates?

SOCRATES: I mean to say that the holy has been acknowledged by us to be loved of God because it is holy, not to be holy because it is loved.

EUTHYPHRO: Yes.

SOCRATES: But that which is dear to the gods is dear to them because it is loved by them, not loved by them because it is dear to them.

EUTHYPHRO: True.

SOCRATES: But, friend Euthyphro, if that which is holy is the same with that which is dear to God, and is loved because it is holy, then that which is dear to God would have been loved as being dear to God; but if that which is dear to God is dear to him because loved by him, then that which is holy would have been holy because loved by him. But now you see that the reverse is the case, and that they are quite different from one another. For one (*theophiles*) is of a kind to be loved cause it is loved, and the other (*osion*) is loved because it is of a kind to be loved. Thus you appear to me, Euthyphro, when I ask you what is the essence of holiness, to offer an attribute only, and not the essence—the attribute of being loved by all the gods. But you still refuse to explain to me the nature of holiness. And therefore, if you please, I will ask you not to hide your treasure, but to tell me once more what holiness or piety really is, whether dear to the gods or not (for that is a matter about which we will not quarrel); and what is impiety?

EUTHYPHRO: I really do not know, Socrates, how to express what I mean. For somehow or other our arguments, on whatever ground we rest them, seem to turn round and walk away from us.

SOCRATES: Your words, Euthyphro, are like the handiwork of my ancestor Daedalus; and if I were the sayer or propounder of them, you might say that my arguments walk away and will not remain fixed where they are placed because I am a descendant of his. But now, since these notions are your own, you must find some other gibe, for they certainly, as you yourself allow, show an inclination to be on the move.

EUTHYPHRO: Nay, Socrates, I shall still say that you are the Daedalus who sets arguments in motion; not I, certainly, but you make them move or go round, for they would never have stirred, as far as I am concerned.

SOCRATES: Then I must be a greater than Daedalus: for whereas he only made his own inventions to move, I move those of other people as well. And the beauty of it is, that I would rather not. For I would give the wisdom of Daedalus, and the wealth of Tantalus, to be able to detain them and keep them fixed. But enough of this. As I perceive that you are lazy, I will myself endeavour to show you how you might instruct me in the nature of piety; and I hope that you will not grudge your labour. Tell me, then—Is not that which is pious necessarily just?

EUTHYPHRO: Yes.

SOCRATES: And is, then, all which is just pious? or, is that which is pious all just, but that which is just, only in part and not all, pious?

EUTHYPHRO: I do not understand you, Socrates.

SOCRATES: And yet I know that you are as much wiser than I am, as you are younger. But, as I was saying, revered friend, the abundance of your wisdom makes you lazy. Please to exert yourself, for there is no real difficulty in understand-

ing me. What I mean I may explain by an illustration of what
I do not mean. The poet [Stasinus] sings—"Of Zeus, the
author and creator of all these things, You will not tell: for
where there is fear there is also reverence." Now I disagree
with this poet. Shall I tell you in what respect?

EUTHYPHRO: By all means.

SOCRATES: I should not say that where there is fear there
is also reverence; for I am sure that many persons fear pov-
erty and disease, and the like evils, but I do not perceive that
they reverence the objects of their fear.

EUTHYPHRO: Very true.

SOCRATES: But where reverence is, there is fear; for he
who has a feeling of reverence and shame about the commis-
sion of any action, fears and is afraid of an ill reputation.

EUTHYPHRO: No doubt.

SOCRATES: Then we are wrong in saying that where
there is fear there is also reverence; and we should say, where
there is reverence there is also fear. But there is not always
reverence where there is fear; for fear is a more extended
notion, and reverence is a part of fear, just as the odd is a part
of number, and number is a more extended notion than the
odd. I suppose that you follow me now?

EUTHYPHRO: Quite well.

SOCRATES: That was the sort of question which I meant
to raise when I asked whether the just is always the pious, or
the pious always the just; and whether there may not be justice where there is not piety; for justice is the more extended
notion of which piety is only a part. Do you dissent?

EUTHYPHRO: No, I think that you are quite right.

SOCRATES: Then, if piety is a part of justice, I suppose
that we should enquire what part? If you had pursued the
enquiry in the previous cases; for instance, if you had asked

me what is an even number, and what part of number the even is, I should have had no difficulty in replying, a number which represents a figure having two equal sides. Do you not agree?

EUTHYPHRO: Yes, I quite agree.

SOCRATES: In like manner, I want you to tell me what part of justice is piety or holiness, that I may be able to tell Meletus not to do me injustice, or indict me for impiety, as I am now adequately instructed by you in the nature of piety or holiness, and their opposites.

EUTHYPHRO: Piety or holiness, Socrates, appears to me to be that part of justice which attends to the gods, as there is the other part of justice which attends to men.

SOCRATES: That is good, Euthyphro; yet still there is a little point about which I should like to have further information. What is the meaning of "attention"? For attention can hardly be used in the same sense when applied to the gods as when applied to other things. For instance, horses are said to require attention, and not every person is able to attend to them, but only a person skilled in horsemanship. Is it not so?

EUTHYPHRO: Certainly.

SOCRATES: I should suppose that the art of horsemanship is the art of attending to horses?

EUTHYPHRO: Yes.

SOCRATES: Nor is every one qualified to attend to dogs, but only the huntsman?

EUTHYPHRO: True.

SOCRATES: And I should also conceive that the art of the huntsman is the art of attending to dogs?

EUTHYPHRO: Yes.

SOCRATES: As the art of the oxherd is the art of attending to oxen?

EUTHYPHRO: Very true.

SOCRATES: In like manner holiness or piety is the art of attending to the gods?—that would be your meaning, Euthyphro?

EUTHYPHRO: Yes.

SOCRATES: And is not attention always designed for the good or benefit of that to which the attention is given? As in the case of horses, you may observe that when attended to by the horseman's art they are benefited and improved, are they not?

EUTHYPHRO: True.

SOCRATES: As the dogs are benefited by the huntsman's art, and the oxen by the art of the oxherd, and all other things are tended or attended for their good and not for their hurt?

EUTHYPHRO: Certainly, not for their hurt.

SOCRATES: But for their good?

EUTHYPHRO: Of course.

SOCRATES: And does piety or holiness, which has been defined to be the art of attending to the gods, benefit or improve them? Would you say that when you do a holy act you make any of the gods better?

EUTHYPHRO: No, no; that was certainly not what I meant.

SOCRATES: And I, Euthyphro, never supposed that you did. I asked you the question about the nature of the attention, because I thought that you did not.

EUTHYPHRO: You do me justice, Socrates; that is not the sort of attention which I mean.

SOCRATES: Good. But I must still ask what is this attention to the gods which is called piety?

EUTHYPHRO: It is such, Socrates, as servants show to their masters.

SOCRATES: I understand—a sort of ministration to the gods.

EUTHYPHRO: Exactly.

SOCRATES: Medicine is also a sort of ministration or service, having in view the attainment of some object—would you not say of health?

EUTHYPHRO: I should.

SOCRATES: Again, there is an art which ministers to the ship-builder with a view to the attainment of some result?

EUTHYPHRO: Yes, Socrates, with a view to the building of a ship.

SOCRATES: As there is an art which ministers to the house-builder with a view to the building of a house?

EUTHYPHRO: Yes.

SOCRATES: And now tell me, my good friend, about the art which ministers to the gods: what work does that help to accomplish? For you must surely know if, as you say, you are of all men living the one who is best instructed in religion.

EUTHYPHRO: And I speak the truth, Socrates.

SOCRATES: Tell me then, oh tell me—what is that fair work which the gods do by the help of our ministrations?

EUTHYPHRO: Many and fair, Socrates, are the works which they do.

SOCRATES: Why, my friend, and so are those of a general. But the chief of them is easily told. Would you not say that victory in war is the chief of them?

EUTHYPHRO: Certainly.

SOCRATES: Many and fair, too, are the works of the husbandman, if I am not mistaken; but his chief work is the production of food from the earth?

EUTHYPHRO: Exactly.

SOCRATES: And of the many and fair things done by the gods, which is the chief or principal one?

EUTHYPHRO: I have told you already, Socrates, that to learn all these things accurately will be very tiresome. Let me simply say that piety or holiness is learning how to please the gods in word and deed, by prayers and sacrifices. Such piety is the salvation of families and states, just as the impious, which is unpleasing to the gods, is their ruin and destruction.

SOCRATES: I think that you could have answered in much fewer words the chief question which I asked, Euthyphro, if you had chosen. But I see plainly that you are not disposed to instruct me—clearly not: else why, when we reached the point, did you turn aside? Had you only answered me I should have truly learned of you by this time the nature of piety. Now, as the asker of a question is necessarily dependent on the answerer, whither he leads I must follow; and can only ask again, what is the pious, and what is piety? Do you mean that they are a sort of science of praying and sacrificing? Do you mean that they are a sort of science of praying and sacrificing?

EUTHYPHRO: Yes, I do.

SOCRATES: And sacrificing is giving to the gods, and prayer is asking of the gods?

EUTHYPHRO: Yes, Socrates.

SOCRATES: Upon this view, then, piety is a science of asking and giving?

EUTHYPHRO: You understand me capitally, Socrates.

SOCRATES: Yes, my friend; the reason is that I am a votary of your science, and give my mind to it, and therefore nothing which you say will be thrown away upon me. Please then to tell me, what is the nature of this service to the gods? Do you mean that we prefer [i.e., put forward] requests and give gifts to them?

EUTHYPHRO: Yes, I do.

SOCRATES: Is not the right way of asking to ask of them what we want?

EUTHYPHRO: Certainly.

SOCRATES: And the right way of giving is to give to them in return what they want of us. There would be no meaning in an art which gives to any one that which he does not want.

EUTHYPHRO: Very true, Socrates.

SOCRATES: Then piety, Euthyphro, is an art which gods and men have of doing business with one another?

EUTHYPHRO: That is an expression which you may use, if you like.

SOCRATES: But I have no particular liking for anything but the truth. I wish, however, that you would tell me what benefit accrues to the gods from our gifts. There is no doubt about what they give to us; for there is no good thing which they do not give; but how we can give any good thing to them in return is far from being equally clear. If they give everything and we give nothing, that must be an affair of business in which we have very greatly the advantage of them.

EUTHYPHRO: And do you imagine, Socrates, that any benefit accrues to the gods from our gifts?

SOCRATES: But if not, Euthyphro, what is the meaning of gifts which are conferred by us upon the gods?

EUTHYPHRO: What else, but tributes of honour; and, as I was just now saying, what pleases them?

SOCRATES: Piety, then, is pleasing to the gods, but not beneficial or dear to them?

EUTHYPHRO: I should say that nothing could be dearer.

SOCRATES: Then once more the assertion is repeated that piety is dear to the gods?

EUTHYPHRO: Certainly.

SOCRATES: And when you say this, can you wonder at your words not standing firm, but walking away? Will you accuse me of being the Daedalus who makes them walk away, not perceiving that there is another and far greater artist than Daedalus who makes them go round in a circle, and he is yourself; for the argument, as you will perceive, comes round to the same point. Were we not saying that the holy or pious was not the same with that which is loved of the gods? Have you forgotten?

EUTHYPHRO: I quite remember.

SOCRATES: And are you not saying that what is loved of the gods is holy; and is not this the same as what is dear to them—do you see?

EUTHYPHRO: True.

SOCRATES: Then either we were wrong in our former assertion; or, if we were right then, we are wrong now.

EUTHYPHRO: One of the two must be true.

SOCRATES: Then we must begin again and ask, What is piety? That is an enquiry which I shall never be weary of pursuing as far as in me lies; and I entreat you not to scorn me, but to apply your mind to the utmost, and tell me the truth. For, if any man knows, you are he; and therefore I must detain you, like Proteus, until you tell. If you had not certainly known the nature of piety and impiety, I am confident that you would never, on behalf of a serf, have charged your aged father with murder. You would not have run such a risk of doing wrong in the sight of the gods, and you would have had too much respect for the opinions of men. I am sure, therefore, that you know the nature of piety and impiety. Speak out then, my dear Euthyphro, and do not hide your knowledge.

EUTHYPHRO: Another time, Socrates; for I am in a hurry, and must go now.

SOCRATES: Alas! My companion, and will you leave me in despair? I was hoping that you would instruct me in the nature of piety and impiety; and then I might have cleared myself of Meletus and his indictment. I would have told him that I had been enlightened by Euthyphro, and had given up rash innovations and speculations, in which I indulged only through ignorance, and that now I am about to lead a better life.

About the Authors

JOHN MÉDAILLE is a former businessman who retired to become an Adjunct Instructor in Theology at the University of Dallas, where he teaches courses in Social Justice for Business Students and Understanding the Bible. He has authored two previous books, *The Vocation of Business: Social Justice in the Marketplace* and *Toward a Truly Free Market: A Distributist Perspective*, and articles in about a dozen other books. He has been married for 48 years, is the father of five, and the grandfather of three. He blogs occasionally at *The Front Porch Republic*.

THOMAS STORCK writes on a wide variety of topics related to Catholic social teaching and Catholic culture and history. He is the author of five previous books, *The Catholic Milieu* (1987), *Foundations of a Catholic Political Order* (1998), *Christendom and the West* (2000), *From Christendom to Americanism and Beyond* (Angelico Press, 2015), and *An Economics of Justice & Charity* (Angelico Press, 2017). Mr. Storck is a member of the editorial board of *The Chesterton Review* and is a contributing editor of *New Oxford Review*. Many of his essays and articles may be found on the website www.thomasstorck.org.